SAVING SIMON

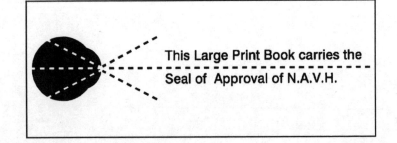

This Large Print Book carries the Seal of Approval of N.A.V.H.

Saving Simon

HOW A RESCUE DONKEY TAUGHT ME THE MEANING OF COMPASSION

Jon Katz

THORNDIKE PRESS
A part of Gale, Cengage Learning

GALE
CENGAGE Learning®

Farmington Hills, Mich • San Francisco • New York • Waterville, Maine
Meriden, Conn • Mason, Ohio • Chicago

GALE
CENGAGE Learning·

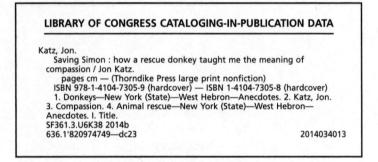

LIBRARY OF CONGRESS CATALOGING-IN-PUBLICATION DATA

Katz, Jon.
    Saving Simon : how a rescue donkey taught me the meaning of compassion / Jon Katz.
        pages cm — (Thorndike Press large print nonfiction)
        ISBN 978-1-4104-7305-9 (hardcover) — ISBN 1-4104-7305-8 (hardcover)
        1. Donkeys—New York (State)—West Hebron—Anecdotes. 2. Katz, Jon. 3. Compassion. 4. Animal rescue—New York (State)—West Hebron—Anecdotes. I. Title.
    SF361.3.U6K38 2014b
    636.1'820974749—dc23   2014034013

Published in 2014 by arrangement with The Ballantine Publishing Group, a division of Random House LLC, a Penguin Random House Company

CONTENTS

■ ■ ■ ■

PART I
SAVING SIMON

■ ■ ■ ■

PROLOGUE:
THE RAID

It was McKenzie Barrett, the animal control officer's daughter, who named him Simon. A name from the Bible, she said, and she thought if she named the donkey Simon he would be blessed and never be hurt again. A New York State Police trooper had come by earlier in the day, climbed the hill nearby with his binoculars, sketched out a map of the donkey's enclosure (he wasn't sure what to call it, it was so small), and distributed copies to everyone assisting with the raid: the other troopers, the vet, the local animal control officer, the driver of the trailer that would take Simon away, dead or alive. It was difficult to tell through the binoculars. He thought it might already be too late.

The property had a farmhouse and a large barn that fronted the north side of the road. Between the house and the old barn, a dirt road — little more than a path at some points — wound back through a meadow and a stand of pine trees, then alongside a small wire mesh enclosure. The structure, completely out of sight from the road, sheltered by brush and trees, was small, the fences sturdy. Even standing by the farmhouse, no one would have imagined it was there.

It was probably built for pigs or a couple of goats — animals that needed strong fences and barriers to keep them contained in a small pen. It was ugly and primitive, a mud path surrounded by heavy mesh fence. Two or three pallets stood up to form a V, low enough for a pig or some chickens to get inside. Through his binoculars the trooper had seen that the donkey was lying down with his head under the pallet, perhaps seeking shelter from the rain. Perhaps to die.

From the slime and muck that coated the creature's side, the trooper saw he had been lying there a long time. His skin was black. They call it rain rot — an animal's skin dying, turning black from lying in the rain and cold for weeks or months and never being dry.

The pallet was an island in a sea of mud, waste, and bits of rotted wood and fence post. The donkey was sunk — stuck, really — in the mud up to his shoulders. He was almost buried in his own manure. The smell was awful, the stench reaching out across the meadow, into the wind.

The trooper estimated the pen was ten feet by ten feet, barely big enough to accommodate the donkey's prone body. If he could stand, the donkey would barely be able to turn around. But he was absolutely still.

Even from the distance, the trooper could see the awful condition of the animal's legs and coat, the skeletal ribs protruding. He could not see any sign of the stomach rising or falling. The animal's home was more like a place to dump garbage or waste, rather than a shelter.

At ten P.M., the trooper was finally at the pen, dreading what he would find. He had fretted about it all day, pushing paperwork, nudging the bureaucracy along, arguing it was worth the time and expense, even though his superiors thought there were more pressing issues.

As the troopers and the animal control officer approached the gate, they stopped. They were hardened and experienced. They had seen a lot, but never anything like this. The animal control officer shook her head. "My God," she said. "Why didn't whoever owns him just shoot him?" One of the young troopers rushed over to the brush and vomited.

The donkey was covered with lice, and tracked with the bite marks of rats. One of the troopers asked the vet how old the donkey was. "There's no way to be sure; I'll have to see him in the light. But I'd guess about fifteen years," the vet replied. He fell silent, shifted his big bag from one shoulder to the other, then said, "Let's get in there."

Rats were spotted at the edge of the field, staring, waiting. A sheriff's deputy put his hand on his gun, but another officer touched his arm, shaking his head. Even rats were not grounds to shoot. He leaned over and tossed a rock out toward the rats, but they did not move.

Another deputy walked up with a light on a tripod stand and a small portable generator. He fired up the generator, and the pen was flooded with white light. The troopers, vet, and animal control officer all gathered around the donkey, who had not moved nor made a sound.

The vet placed the flat metal disc of his stethoscope on the donkey's neck. "Well, he's alive," he said. "Barely. Let's get the pallet off of him."

They stood up and shifted the wooden

structure away from the donkey's head and shined their flashlights on his face. There was a moment of stunned silence, then some of the men tied handkerchiefs over their noses and everybody got to work.

The vet placed his big canvas bag down in the mud, taking out syringes, vials, sponges, painkillers, wrenches and clamps for teeth pulling, vitamins and energy boosters, balm and ointments for the skin, powder for the lice, gauze patches for the rat bites, antibiotics for the oozing eyes. What to treat first? He would need everything he had. He went to work quickly.

The troopers were used to standing and watching and waiting. It was a big part of the job. They gathered in a circle behind the vet, handing him towels and blankets, hand wipes and tools, pointing their flashlights where he asked. Some of the work he could do later, after they transported the donkey to the animal control officer's farm a few towns over. That was the plan. If Simon was still alive, they would stabilize him and get him up and over to the farm. There was a barn there with some empty stalls. They could get a better look at him in the morning.

As the vet kneeled over the donkey, he said, "This is the worst state I have ever seen an animal in in twenty years of practice." He was surprised to see his own tears falling on his bag, on his bottles and wraps. It rarely happened, but he told himself to suck it up and get to work. Lord, he thought, I did not ever want to see this. But wasn't it why he had become a vet, wasn't it the point? Sometimes, he thought, I am ashamed to be a human.

He had little time. The animal's pulse and heartbeat were fading quickly.

The vet had seen that the donkey's hooves were sticking out like wings, it had been so long since they were trimmed. "He must have been walking on his ankles," he said. "He can't walk that way to the trailer. I have to cut the hooves off right now."

He stood, ran over to his truck, and pulled out a battery-charged buzz saw.

He reached for the painkillers and a sedative. He would have to put the donkey out for a bit. The pain must be horrible. But if he didn't trim his hooves, he would never make it to the trailer.

Before he started, he pulled open the donkey's mouth. Simon's right eye was sticking out of the mud, open, staring at him through the film and ooze. The vet looked at his jaw, then up at the trooper. "I have to pull them now, there's a massive infection in there. I have to sedate him. I won't knock him out, because we won't be able to get him up. I'll get him sleepy, poor guy, but he's going to feel this." And he went to work.

"Will he make it?" asked one of the troopers.

"I don't know," said the vet. "A part of me thinks he ought not to make it; that would give him some peace."

"No," said the animal control officer, leaning over, putting her arm on the vet's shoulder. "I think I may have found a home for him. A guy has two donkeys, a writer. He said he'd come take a look in the morning, if we can get him to my house. Let's try it, let's give him a shot."

The vet looked up at her, nodded. He opened Simon's jaws and put a clamp inside to keep them open.

They did not know a donkey could scream.

He would have died except for the child who lived in the farmhouse. The small boy came quietly every night, very late. Simon could have seen his face clearly in the moonlight if he had been watching for him, but mostly he became aware of him as he approached the fence, so softly in his bare feet, even in the cold, whispering quietly for Simon to be still, and tossing some hay over the fence toward the donkey's head.

At first, the boy could reach over the fence and hold some hay out for Simon to grasp, but in recent days, Simon was lying on his side, unable to move or stand up, and the boy threw the hay as near to Simon's head as he could.

"I'm sorry," the boy would say, sometimes crying. "This is all that I can give you. I can't do any more." He would look to see if the donkey were still alive, toss the hay, then as quickly as he had come, he was gone, vanished into the meadows behind the farmhouse. From the first, Simon loved the boy, as donkeys so dearly love their human children. They protect them, watch for them, bray softly for them, love giving them rides on their backs and hanging around them. The spirits of children are so like the spirits of donkeys, small and good and open, curious and independent.

The boy had always sensed that Simon needed human attention. For all the hard things that came from people, donkeys never take attention for granted. They need the touch of people, the safety and the tenderness of children. It heals them, and they heal in return.

■ ■ ■ ■

Simon was still. The vet was finishing his work and the animal control officer had begun to think about Simon's future. "We need to try. That writer texted again; he has a big barn and lots of pasture. He loves animals and he's stubborn like a donkey. They'll get along."

And then, unimaginably just a few minutes later, Simon was moving, his instincts returning, fighting to live.

The animal control officer — she had long yellow hair, the kind donkeys love to nibble on — and the men were all shouting at him: "Simon, get up! Get up! You're okay now! We're here to take you away!" They were excited, and their excitement was being transmitted to him. The vet kept yelling that his pulse was dropping. He was in shock. They forced open his swollen jaws again and squirted liquid into his stomach through a tube. They put a needle in his neck and attached it to a plastic bottle hanging on a stand.

"Eat it, Simon," they begged, "eat it. Get up, move, please move." Simon started at the radios crackling; in numbing pain, he was blinded by the bright and flashing lights and confused by the noise. He seemed dizzy, light-headed and struggling. He seemed to focus on one person, the woman with the blond hair. She had connected with him; it was as if she grounded him, helped him make sense of the chaos and pain.

They made their way slowly down the drive, and then the procession suddenly stopped.

Across from the farmhouse, his hands folded across his chest, his head bowed, the farmer stood waiting. The troopers and the others stopped to look at him. Some were angry — it showed on their faces. Others were bewildered, trying to comprehend. The farmer looked exhausted, downcast. He was in jeans, wearing heavy boots and a red flannel shirt. He could not lift his eyes to look at Simon. The troopers went over to him, said something, handed him some paper.

"I'm sorry," said the farmer, still looking down. "Things got away from me. After a while, I just couldn't bear to go back there. I couldn't stand to see it."

The troopers said nothing; they just stared back at him.

Walking back toward Simon, one trooper turned to the other and said, "I've seen it before. They just can't ask for help, can't admit when they're so far down." The other trooper nodded.

They shined their powerful flashlights into the darkness. The bushes stirred and the boy came out, in his pajamas, barefoot in the mud and cold. The boy was short, thin, about ten years old, a mop of brown hair hanging over his face. His eyes were red and moist.

"What are you doing in there, son?" asked one of the troopers. The boy edged forward toward Simon and the trooper moved to stop him. The animal control officer waved the trooper back and took the boy's hand. She leaned over and whispered something in his ear, tousled his hair. "You're the one who called." It was a statement, not a question.

"Don't worry," said the woman. "It's our secret. Do you want to say good-bye?"

The boy looked up at her and Simon, and nodded. "Please," he said, looking anxiously back at the farmhouse. Simon's ears went up; he brayed softly. Even the animal seemed startled by the weak, squeaky sound, more fitting for a mouse than a donkey.

The boy looked at Simon, then at the troopers. "My dad is a good man," he told the big sergeant. "It's just hard now."

The sergeant nodded.

Simon seemed so at ease with the boy that

the animal control officer turned over the reins to the child. The boy, smiling now, took the lead and called out to Simon, "C'mon, let's go," and the procession resumed. He led Simon down the path and onto the road and right up into the trailer, although it took Simon a long time to get up the ramp on his painful and unsteady legs. When he did, helped along by half a dozen pairs of strong arms, the boy was waiting for him, holding a leaf of hay. Simon stood for a bit, taking the hay into his mouth, eager for its rich and warm taste, even with his painful gums and swollen jaw.

The boy reached up and hugged Simon, kissing him on the nose. Simon watched him walk down the trailer ramp. He turned to follow but he could not, restrained now by gates and ropes tied to rings in the corners of the trailer.

The boy turned and waved, then ran off. Simon's plaintive bray echoed off the trailer walls and out into the meadow, and over that small and awful place that had been his home — the home he would never see again.

Simon was tied firmly to the trailer sides, but it bumped over dirt roads and wobbled back and forth, and each bump and turn was like a bolt of lightning up his legs, into his jaw. They stood alongside him, talking to him, rubbing salve onto his wounds, telling him it would be okay. Soon the trailer came to a new place. Simon was led off to a large red barn. He heard horses neighing to him from the pasture beyond. He felt the jabs of more needles, then, drained and exhausted, he collapsed onto a bed of straw.

They worked through the night to save him. They finished sawing the wings off of his feet. They pulled half of his teeth, the infected ones, from his jaw. He was bathed in medicines to heal the sores; powders were applied to kill the lice and fleas. They put braces on his legs to hold them, drops in his eyes to clear them, gauze poultices to reduce the swelling in his mouth. Wounds were wrapped and medicines administered to heal the rat bites. The rain rot, his blackened skin, would take months to heal. Simon's legs would never be completely straight, but with luck, he might be able to walk and move around.

Outside, the troopers sat in their cars, their engines idling, drinking their coffee, passing updates back and forth. People often get wrapped up in the fates of animals, and these men were no exception. They were invested in saving this beat-up old donkey, left for dead in his pen, even though none of them was likely to ever see him again. That was the nature of their work. "Will he make it?" one asked. "You have to admire him," said another. "He never quit. Think what it must have taken to stay alive in that hellhole."

By the late morning, the troopers had left, and Simon was alone again. He looked around. He was under shelter, but the gates were open, and next to him was a small field filled with shrubs. It was early spring and the grass had started to come up. Simon staggered over to it, leaned his head down, and seemed to almost drink up the moist, fresh grass, the lifeblood of the donkey. Then he lay down.

It was quiet; the birds were singing. Cars and trucks whizzed down a busy highway. He listened to the dogs barking nearby, was aware of horses in a pasture up the hill.

There was hay all around him, and a bed of straw to lie on. His eyes were clearing; he could see again. A few feet down the hill, there was a creek with fresh water, and he gathered himself to get down to it to drink greedily and for a long time.

His stomach ached, but he was not really

hungry. There was nothing familiar around him. He brayed, calling out to the boy, but he was not there; he did not come.

ONE:
MY FIRST DONKEY

I ought to explain why it was that the police thought I might take a dying donkey onto my farm, an unusual thing for a city boy like me, who, for most of my life, thought that donkeys lived only in India or Spain.

I asked the animal control officer how many people they had asked to consider taking Simon, wondering how I had come to her attention and that of the New York State Police. "Just you," she said.

"Oh," I said in one of those mind-altering moments when you get a glimpse of how others might see you.

"We knew you had some donkeys and loved them," she said. "I read your books."

I'm an author and photographer who owns a farm in upstate New York. I live there with my wife, Maria, and numerous animals. My life has never proceeded in straight lines; zigs and zags are more my style. If my life on a farm is characterized by any one idea, it would be this: one thing leads to another.

And it was Carol that led, in zigs and zags, to Simon.

I believe the first donkey I ever laid eyes on was wearing a straw hat and hee-hawing at Elmer Fudd in a Saturday morning cartoon. I remember the donkey had enormous teeth and was rather loud and goofy.

I never saw a real donkey until I was nearly fifty years old. I had taken my border collie out to a sheep farm in Pennsylvania to learn how to herd sheep. The experience transformed me in many ways. I decided to buy my own farm, I began writing about dogs, and I encountered a donkey who was to alter the nature of my life.

Carol was nearly twenty years old when I met her. She was living in a small corral. Like many donkeys, Carol seemed an afterthought, a misfit. Donkeys come to farms for all kinds of reasons. Somebody might trade a donkey for an old horse or for some hay. A farmer might come across one and take pity on it, or suspect it might be useful down the road.

Sometimes donkeys luck out and end up on rich horse farms, keeping horses company, getting to eat the good hay and grain, and are even quartered indoors in heated stalls. But that is not the fate of most donkeys. Donkeys have lived with humans as long as or longer than dogs have, but donkeys haven't figured out how to worm their way into human hearts quite so well. Their history and general treatment do not speak well of the generosity and mercy of human beings.

The farmer couldn't even quite remember how Carol had ended up with him but she had been in that corral every day for the sixteen years that he had owned her. Once in a while he tossed some hay over the fence and filled up the rusty bathtub with fresh water, but mostly, Carol survived off of brush and bark, pooled rain water, and water from a small muddy stream that ran through her corral. Twice a year, a farrier came to trim her hooves.

The farmer was busy, and he conceded that most of the time, he forgot about Carol. Farm animals are not pets; they are pretty hardy. Donkeys are especially hardy, and can go far on very little.

The thought of Carol alone for years in that tiny patch of woods haunted me, offering some of the first stirrings of an emotional notion of compassion, but even then, my response to her was to bring some apples whenever I visited the farm; it didn't go much deeper than that. I was distracted, busy, I had a kid, other worries; the life of a donkey seemed very remote to me.

Carol was not good-natured or accepting, and she did not wish to have her hooves trimmed. After a while, the battered farrier just gave her a drugged apple before going to work. She still managed to bite and kick him at least once every time. The farmer told me this by way of cautioning me to be careful around her. "She has sweet eyes," he said, "but she is not sweet." Maybe, I thought, that was why he had left her alone in that corral all these years.

Carol's corral was right next to the big pasture where I was learning to herd sheep with my dog, and I would see her staring at me. It unnerved me. She seemed to be trying to tell me something, but since I had never come near a real donkey in my life, I had no idea what it was she might be saying.

I felt bad for her, in the way middle-class people who grew up in cities feel bad for animals who live their natural lives out in the real world. We just can't help but project feelings into their heads. I just assumed she was hungry, and she seemed quite lonely all by herself in that corral, staring at me.

The first time I brought her apples, I

34

walked over to the corral, my pockets stuffed with some big, red, juicy ones. Carol leaned over the fence, grabbed the first apple — and nearly my thumb with it — and crunched it judiciously and hungrily. My dog was standing back, staring at Carol, trying to keep an eye on the sheep who were grazing nearby.

I reached for another apple, but Carol was not willing to be patient. She walked right through the fence, dragging wire and fence posts behind her, put her ears down, and charged my terrified dog, who took off toward the other side of the pasture. The sheep needed no invitation to leave, and they took off in the other direction. Carol then turned to me, ripped the apple out of my pocket, and began nosing my other pockets for more.

"Hey, hey," I said, not sure what commands to give a donkey. I was shocked to realize she could have walked through the fence any day of those sixteen years she had spent there had she chosen to. It was my first real demonstration of donkey thinking. The first rule of the donkey ethos: everything is their idea.

It took a while for the irritated farmer to get Carol back inside — a loaf of bread did it — and he warned me in no uncertain terms to leave her alone.

I couldn't do that, of course. Every time I came herding, I brought apples and carrots. I would climb into her corral with the treats so she would have no reason to bust out.

There are some people who are deeply drawn into the rescue of animals. I am not one. I think in some ways animal rescue is too intense for me, too difficult. Perhaps that's one reason I love happy, healthy, well-bred working dogs. I love to do things with them; I love the way they enter my life easily and come along with me.

But I fell in love with Carol, this grumpy, independent creature. I worried about her. I wanted to help her. It did something for me — something selfish — to treat her well. It fed something inside of me.

In her own way, she was quite affectionate with me. She loved it when I rubbed the inside of her ears or tickled the sides of her nose. She would not let me brush her, and if I didn't have an apple, she would lower her head and butt me in the side or rear end. Carol made no pretense about our relationship — she wanted the apples, and if she felt like it, she might allow me to show her some affection. Or not. Donkeys cannot be bought or bribed, only appeased.

And Carol . . . well, she was not very nice.

She wouldn't have fit into one of those cute donkey tales in cartoons and movies. Sometimes you had to like the idea of her more than Carol herself. This was perhaps the first inkling I had about the vagaries of compassion — we tend to feel it for people and animals we like; it is hard to feel it for people and animals we don't like.

Whenever I was out herding, Carol would come over to the fence and hang her head on the outside, her ears turning like radar scanners, eyeing me soulfully with her big brown eyes. Somehow, it seemed as if I were her human, and she was my donkey, even though my home at the time was in suburban New Jersey, where donkeys played no part in the life of anyone.

A year or so after I met Carol, I bought a farm in upstate New York — I called it Bedlam Farm — and I bought some of the sheep I had been working with. The farmer hired somebody with a trailer to drive them up to me. If I had never met a donkey before Carol, I also had never set foot on a farm before in my life — I was raised in Providence, Rhode Island, and had lived in New York City, Dallas, Boston, Washington, and Baltimore before moving to New Jersey. The farm would, in my mind, become a laboratory for my newfound passion to write about dogs, animals, and rural life. Bedlam Farm consisted of ninety acres, a Civil War-era farmhouse, four barns, and large areas of fenced-in pasture. It was a good place for sheep and a paradise for donkeys, although I had no plans to acquire any. I had heard from farmers that donkeys were wonderful guard animals, and would keep coyotes and predators away from sheep. But I had my hands full just trying to survive on my new farm. When the trailer of sheep arrived, the driver backed it into the pasture and opened the gates.

The first creature out was Carol, who looked around disdainfully, snorted, kicked one of the sheep away from her, and put her nose in my pocket. The driver handed me a note from the farmer, which read, "Here is Carol. You love her so much, you can feed her."

So began my life with Carol. She was, from the first, the most imperious creature I had ever met, human or animal. In hot summers, she loved to hang out in the big shady barn. She could hardly believe her good fortune having acres of pasture to wander and all the grass and fresh water she might want.

Carol was an older donkey, and she had lived outdoors for years without shelter or good, nutritious food. I saw her limping, and had a large-animal vet come and check her out. Carol did not wish to be examined. She butted the vet into the wall, tried to bite him, and nearly kicked him through the window. We got a halter on her and cross-tied her to the sides of the barn. She had a laundry list of ailments, from foundering — a painful wasting disease of the hooves — to swollen joints and gums. She was, the vet said, in great pain, and he gave her some shots and handed me a bunch of long needles to stick in her butt later in the day. Then he left.

That night, when I went out to administer the medications, I got another major lesson in donkey thinking. They read intentions. When I came out to give Carol an apple, she was standing by the gate, meek as a kitten. If I came out with some needles or medicines in my pocket, she was off and running. That night it was –20°F, and a stubborn human and a stubborn donkey had an epic confrontation on my farm's hilly pasture. Carol took off in a blinding storm, hobbling and stumbling up a hill, as my border collie Rose and I gave chase. I caught her an hour later on the top of the hill and stuck the needle in her butt while she dragged me all the way back down the hill. I got frostbite in three fingers that night. I learned that if you want to give a donkey a needle, get her in a small stall with a grain bucket, hide the needle out of sight, and then stick her when her mouth is full.

Despite all her ailments, she kept giving me donkey lessons.

One was the gate lesson. You can't just have a normal gate with a donkey. I had a chain that hung on my gate and when you closed it, you wrapped the chain around the gatepost and it held fast. Carol loved to open gates and doors and windows; it was child's play for her. It took me a while to figure it out, but she would watch me latch the gate, then she would lean over the fence and unwrap the chain, and the gate would swing open. Twice, I came home to find that the gate was open, and so was the back door of the farmhouse — the knob was fun for her to grab and twist. Carol would get into the kitchen, open the cabinets, and munch on bread and cereal. And it was not simple to get her out of the kitchen, either, no matter how loudly I would stomp my feet and yell.

The only thing that drove her out was when I banged some pans together, startling her. Donkeys do not like loud sounds. Carol pretty much went where she pleased, until I spent some serious money on latches that could not be opened from the inside.

Still, Carol taught me much about love, or the very special ways in which donkeys love.

Carol's hooves and health were stabilized for a while with vitamins, special grain, leg wraps, daily shots (administered bravely by me), painkillers, and the best hay. That winter, there was too much ice and snow for her to make it up to the hill, her favorite spot for avoiding me, so we really got to know each other.

I had to go into the barn every night to give Carol all of her many medicines and wraps, and that took the better part of an hour. I worked out a deal with her. If I brought a bucket of grain or oats or something wonderful to eat, she would become surprisingly tolerant of my sticking needles into her and forcing pills down her big, smelly mouth. If I didn't, the process was war from beginning to end.

It wasn't that she was bribable — she was not — but as a donkey who had lived off of grass, the bark of trees, and old hay, she seemed to consider it a good deal to get her oats in exchange for some intrusive prodding and poking. I like to think she came to trust me, but I will also admit I bought a lot of good grain. Carol loved to eat, sniffing her food, picking it up in small amounts, chewing it deliberately, savoring each morsel. What was a needle in the face of that?

I made another surprising discovery. Carol loved music and, more than anything, she loved Willie Nelson. I like Willie Nelson, too, and I discovered this shared passion when I brought a boom box into the barn with me to play while I was sorting through Carol's large bucket of pills and treatments.

When I played "Georgia on My Mind," Carol's lip quivered — this is how donkeys show contentment — and her eyes closed and she just seemed calm and serene. I came to love those moments — the big barn creaking in the wind, the barn cats skittering around the hay bales, Willie Nelson's gravelly but soothing voice echoing off the big old rafters in the roof. The music connected us somehow. It got to Carol, reached some unfathomable part of her.

I got some greatest hits albums — she especially loved "Good Hearted Woman," "Momma, Don't Let Your Babies Grow Up to Be Cowboys," and "Help Me Make It Through the Night."

Those hours in the barn became special to both of us. She would listen to Willie Nelson, who would put her into a mellow and dreamy state, and I would chew my granola bar — I thought we should be eating oats together — and those sessions became sweet, calm, and healing for both of us.

Carol grew stronger and heartier, and I think she looked forward to our evenings as much as I did. Donkey bonding, I guess you'd call it. After a while, I began talking to her, and she seemed to be listening to me.

I came to admire Carol for her integrity, her independence, and, eventually, the affection she would show me, leaning against me, letting me brush and stroke her forehead. Carol started to matter to me. She wasn't just an animal I was taking care of; we had connected in a deep way — a way I had not experienced before. It was different from what I'd had with dogs or other pets. It felt like something old, almost mystical.

A few months after Carol came to my farm, I got a telephone call from a woman who said she had driven by the farm and observed Carol. She wanted to tell me, she said, that Carol was troubled. That she did not know she was a donkey; she was not in touch with her "donkeyness." This was a bit of a shock to me. It was not something I had thought much about, yet it did click. Carol had spent most of her life alone in that farm corral in Pennsylvania. She may not have ever seen another donkey.

Who, I asked the woman, might you be?

"I am a Jewish donkey spiritualist," said the woman, introducing her self as Pat Freund. She bred and raised donkeys on her farm nearby and she suggested that I come and see them, and perhaps take one home to keep Carol company. They were herd animals, she said. They needed to be with other donkeys.

Pat came to the farm, and she was everything she said she was. She and Carol touched heads and communicated with each other. I visited Pat's farm and went into her barn, which was filled with beautiful donkeys of all ages, gliding around me.

A few days later, Fanny arrived, and Carol flipped out, going into the barn for a week and refusing to come out, although she still ate her bucket of grain and listened to Willie Nelson at night with me.

She was clearly rattled. When she did come out, she was different.

She had, in fact, come to terms with her "donkeyness." You could see it. She and Fanny were inseparable from that moment, always within a few feet of each other. Carol now knew who she was. She was a donkey.

Although Fanny didn't seem to get Willie Nelson, she was happy to join our evenings, eating some grain alongside Carol while I tended to the old donkey's wounds and cranked up "Help Me Make It Through the Night."

A few months after Fanny arrived, Pat Freund called to tell me that Fanny's sister was for sale, and Lulu came to the farm. My donkeys became a happy threesome.

That winter, I saw Lulu and Fanny standing alone by the big barn. They looked agitated, and I looked around for Carol. I found her up in the pole barn. She seemed dazed, walking in circles and bumping her head on the barn's wooden sides. The vet came and said she had had a stroke. Carol legs had been weakening lately and now it was hard for her to stand.

For most animal lovers, especially people with pets, compassion means keeping animals alive, going into debt sometimes, taking every step, making every commitment to extend life. This is, to many, the very definition of love.

I turned to the large-animal vet when he examined Carol, and I asked what would be the most compassionate thing to do. He put his hand on my shoulder. "Oh," he said, "that is pretty simple. We should put her down."

Simple? Nothing about compassion is

simple in our world, especially the idea that ending a life can be more merciful than prolonging it. But I agreed. I didn't need any further discussion.

I was glad to have given Carol a few great years. She loved her life on the farm, especially the green grass in the summer and fresh hay in the winter. As her body lay by the pasture gate, Lulu and Fanny came over to sniff her, and I played Willie on the boom box singing "Blue Eyes Crying in the Rain."

It was raining that day, and I did a good bit of crying in the rain myself. But my life with donkeys was under way.

Two:
Simon Arrives

On a warm spring Sunday in April 2011, the battered trailer bringing Simon to Bedlam Farm backed up our steep driveway. Jessica Barrett, the animal control officer, and her husband, Chris, got out and we agreed to place Simon by himself in the rear pasture behind the big barn. Their daughter McKenzie, who had helped pull Simon back to life, was there also. She had bonded with Simon at their farm. When they let him out of the trailer, Simon could not take his eyes off McKenzie; it was as if she was the only thing his battered instincts could focus on.

He followed her around the pasture, although he hobbled every step of the way and seemed disoriented. Jessica said she could not imagine the pain he was in.

We knew we had to keep Simon away from the other donkeys. These animals can be gentle, but they can also be mean-spirited, ungenerous, and less than gracious when it comes to making room for strangers or sharing their food. Equines often greet new members of a herd with kicks and bites, and Simon could not have withstood any of that.

Simon was also a male, and I knew from my time on the farm that males behaved differently from females, and females behaved differently around them.

I knew there would eventually be some considerable butting and kicking and jockeying, even though Simon was a gelded male. But at this point, he was far too weak to engage in animal politics — a sharp kick or head butt or bite could have killed him.

Lulu and Fanny were inseparable and peaceable, but it would take a while before they got used to sharing their food, treats, pasture, and humans. They were also wise to the ways of trailers. Donkeys do not like to go places in moving vehicles — it rarely leads to good things for them — and so they stood well up the hill watching.

Even though I had seen Simon the day before, I was once again shocked by his blackened skin, his twisted legs, his clouded eyes and emaciated legs and ribs. As a former police reporter, I have a good idea of what humans are capable of, but the sight of Simon drove it home in a painfully direct way. He made me want to cry for all of us.

I felt somehow connected to Simon's experience of aloneness and confusion, of fear and discomfort. I had spent a lot of my life that way. I seemed to know where Simon hurt, and I seemed to know what he needed — how to make him feel better.

My wife, Maria, and I took turns giving him medications, cleaning him, feeding him, administering his painkillers, and applying his potions and creams. But she was not as affected by him as I was, nor was he as connected to her. Something in me connected with something in him, but it was something I could not yet define. It wasn't an intellectual reaction; it was an emotional one. I knew I had to bring him back, heal him, to reaffirm the better parts of being human.

The rear pasture was about seven acres and had the lushest, greenest grass on the farm. There was a covered hay feeder near the gate that provided shelter for the hay during rain and snow, as well as shade for the animals. A one-acre corral surrounded the feeder and sealed the area off from the larger pasture. I used it for lambing. There was a large door leading to the big barn where Simon could go to get away from the flies, if there was a lot of rain and mud, or if he got too hot and wanted to cool off.

He was too weak to mount much of a defense against the voracious horseflies that torment livestock in the summer. We were concerned that flies and maggots could get into his wounds and sores. He was weak, and the vet said he had little or no resistance to bacteria and infection. It would take weeks, even months, to build up his immune system.

So Simon needed to have plenty of shelter, and to have his wounds checked several times a day. We bought gallons of thick black balm to keep insects off of him, and tubes of antibiotics. We had to be careful about feeding him. Like humans who have been starved or malnourished, he couldn't handle a rich, full diet. I'd have to hand-feed hay to him until we could trust him to eat what he chose.

On that first morning, it took Simon a long time to walk the fifteen yards or so to the covered hay feeder and then, spent, he collapsed on the ground. Jessica, Chris, and McKenzie said good-bye, handed me a bucket of salves and other medications, and left. They would come back in a few weeks, they said, with some adoption papers if we decided to keep him.

I think Simon decided from the first that he would live. It's what donkeys do: endure hard times and keep going. That is surely their history. My first days with Simon are a blur. Maria and I moved back and forth from the house to the barn all day, ferrying water, medicines, hay, carrots, apples, oat cookies, balms and salves, anti-fly sprays and ointments.

It turned out that our farrier, Ken Norman, a big, gruff, profoundly gentle man, had gone to Jessica Barrett's farm to work on Simon's hooves when he was first taken out of his pen. He said it was one of the worst things he had ever seen done to an animal — that the hooves had grown out nearly a foot on either side and that Simon was walking on his ankles.

Ken came by to check on Simon, and to trim his hooves a little further — Simon was too beat up to endure much more work at the moment. I was told his legs would never be straight, and walking might always be painful. But he was a good boy, Ken said, and he wanted to live.

In those first few days, I wasn't sure he would. Simon was usually lying down under the covered hay feeder when Maria and I came out. He was gentle and trusting. He did not resist the many ointments, pills, and salves we tormented him with for days and weeks. We had to make sure the flies stayed off him, that the wounds healed without infection, and that he had soft food that wouldn't challenge his healing gums. Many of his teeth had literally grown into his jaw, he had been lying on his side for so long, and they had been removed. He had most of his front teeth, but chewing was difficult for him, and still painful.

Since walking was also difficult, I pulled up fresh grass and piled it next to him, and brought him some hay from the bales in the barn. He had terrible diarrhea those first few days, and the evidence of that was all around the feeder.

Simon watched me closely; his big brown eyes were always on me. How could I help him, I wondered. What did he need?

I've lived with animals for years, seen them born and die, get sick and heal, get sick and die. I have always kept some distance from the animal rescue culture. I resist seeing animals as piteous and abused creatures — it is a prism that is too narrow for me. But I had never seen anything quite like Simon, an animal in such extreme distress and suffering. I felt it rearrange my heart, penetrate it, unleash old anger, hurt, fear.

I think part of my problem with the rescue culture is that I don't like to see myself as piteous and abused, either, and yet to a large extent, I was, and I had been working to heal those wounds my entire life, and to move beyond them.

And here those wounds were right in front of me, lying on the ground, needing me to rub all kinds of pastes and oils and balms on them, to massage them, knead them, inspect them. It was a shockingly intimate experience for me, and it engaged the deepest and most private and painful parts of me. Simon made me see myself in a jarring, intensely emotional way.

I felt an enormous pull to bring this animal back to life. We would not lose this one. This creature would not be sacrificed to the inexplicable inhumanity and cruelty of human beings.

There is something about the mistreatment of children and of animals — helpless beings, in so many ways — that stands out in the spectrum of human failings.

Lying down on the ground, in the mud, in the waste and vomit that spewed out of

Simon, hand-feeding him hay, gagging on the smell and maggots, fending off the savage horseflies, I felt right away that I was knee-deep, not only in the broken and open wounds of Simon, but of me.

Something about the way Simon looked at me, the intense focus of those big brown eyes, spoke to me. There was trust in that look, and great interest. Perhaps not affection, not yet. I was too new and strange for him, and he was too disabled and stunned. But a part of each of us had found the other.

If I could help Simon heal, maybe he could help heal me. A grand bargain.

The second night Simon was with us, I thought back to Carol and how much she had seemed to love listening to Willie Nelson with me. Donkeys, I had seen, need people in much the same way dogs do. They have been living with people for so many thousands of years. Whenever a donkey meets a human, they first look for some food — an offering or tribute, a cookie, a carrot, or an apple.

But then, satisfied with their deal, rewarded for their time, they always — always — offer something back. They press themselves against you and allow themselves to be touched, brushed, even kissed on the nose.

What might Simon and I do together? Where might we go? What might our story be? I wondered, what could I offer him beyond food and medicine? What might we share?

As it happened, I had the first part of my answer waiting on my bookshelf, right on the farm.

Considered a masterpiece, *Platero and I* is a lyrical, even magical, portrait of life in a remote Andalusian village in Spain. Its author, the Spanish poet Juan Ramón Jiménez, was awarded the 1956 Nobel Prize for Literature.

Jiménez and Platero, his gentle donkey, travel through the tiny Andalusian town of Moguer and the beautiful country lanes beyond, Jiménez speaking of the sights and sounds that touch and inspire him — white butterflies, sparrows, an old building, ripe pomegranates — and of human emotions of love, fear, nostalgia, and longing.

Platero is a small downy donkey who loves mandarin oranges, grapes, and "purple figs tipped with crystalline drops of honey." He is, writes Jiménez, as loving and tender as a child, as strong and sturdy as a rock.

Someone gave me *Platero and I* as a gift

after Carol died, and it seemed that Jiménez captured more gracefully and sweetly than anyone I had read before the great duality of donkeys — they are the most gentle and loving of creatures, and also the hardiest and most determined and willful. In my own life with animals, I have encountered none who embody that contradiction as powerfully as donkeys. There is no end to the amount of work we ask them to do, and their great hearts seem to forgive us the most unimaginable insults and cruelty.

To the people of Moguer, Platero is "like steel," but the poet corrects them. "Steel, yes," he tells them, "steel and moon silver." This, it struck me, was Simon. Only a creature of steel would have still been alive, yet the moon silver was already shining through in him.

I took my dog-eared copy of *Platero and I* and some carrots and I headed out into the back pasture where Simon was sitting up, gazing out at the valley below. He seemed to be paying particular attention to the huge full moon hovering out over the valley.

He turned to look at me, as he always did when I came near, and I thought I heard a soft bray coming from him as I got closer. Donkeys have a sixth sense about treats, and I guessed he smelled the carrots in my pocket or perhaps saw one sticking out. I had brought a blanket, and I laid it down beside him. I changed his dressings, applied his ointments, gave him his pills, and squirted syringes full of medicine through an opening in his jaw. I brought him fresh hay and water, checked for lice and maggots, and squirted medicine into his eyes.

Simon was almost shockingly gracious about all of this. I knew Carol would have butted me all over the barnyard by now, sick or not. Miraculously, something in Simon loved and trusted people. Animals don't do self-pity or revenge, certainly not donkeys, who have endured the harshest treatment and retain their genial and affectionate nature. If you study the brutal history of donkeys and their lives serving people, you wonder why any donkey would go near any human being, but that is, of course, a projection. They are not like us.

They don't have expectations and do not flirt with disappointment.

When the ministrations were over and Simon had eaten his hay and cookies, chewed his carrot, and taken his medicine, I took out a reading light and clamped it to *Platero and I*.

"Look, Simon," I recall telling him. "This is a story about a man and his donkey.

Every night, I'm going to come out here and read you a different story from this book. I hope you'll like it."

Simon and I looked out over the valley for a minute, and I wondered what was going through the mind of this battered creature. Many people think they know what is in the minds of animals, but the longer I live with them, the less certain I am of what they are thinking. Simon was not, I am sure, aware of the drama of his life.

Yesterday he was suffering and starving; today he was not. He seemed to relish his view over the valley. The shade of the feeder gave him some protection from the flies and gnats. We covered the barn floor with straw, and as soon as he was strong enough, we hoped to get him inside, but for now, the softer ground outside seemed more comfortable than the concrete of the barn.

He seemed at ease in my presence. This was somebody's donkey, I thought. He was used to people — trusted them still.

A soft breeze came up from the valley. We paused to drink it in, both of us at ease. I brought a bottle of water to sip, and I saw my border collie Rose come cautiously into the barn and sit to watch us.

Rose had been living with donkeys for a couple of years, and she had a great deal of respect for the distance she wanted to keep from them. Up on the hill, I saw Lulu and Fanny standing by the gate, staring at us. Donkeys are alert creatures. They miss nothing, and Lulu and Fanny had become Simon scholars, studying every minute of his life and treatment. It would be many weeks before the three would get together, and then only after a slow and deliberate process of acclimation.

How curious life is, I thought, that I would be sitting out in a pasture getting ready to read to a donkey I barely knew.

When we had all settled, and the sun was sinking below the mountains, I read Simon the opening paragraphs of *Platero and I:* "Platero is a small donkey, a soft, hairy donkey: so soft to the touch that he might be said to be made of cotton, with no bones. Only the jet mirrors of his eyes are hard like two black crystal scarabs."

When he called to Platero softly, wrote Jiménez, he came "at a gay little trot that is like laughter of a vague, idyllic, tinkling sound."

Jiménez and Platero had begun their journey through beautiful Andalusia, and Simon and I had begun our own.

We had just had our first real conversation, our first moment together. If Simon did not know what the story's words meant, I have no doubt he was reading my tone of voice. He understood, I am sure, that I was offering him an invitation into my life, my journey.

As I read him the first pages of *Platero*, I noticed that Simon never took his eyes off me. His blackened ears swiveled to catch the words, but, more important, the intonations and the feeling behind them.

I had heard, and then learned, that you cannot fool a donkey: He will see right into your heart and right through deceit and prevarication. He knows where you are going before you do.

I felt that night that Simon accepted my invitation. I was excited to join the glorious fraternity of strange men who roamed the world observing it and sharing it with their donkeys.

"Simon," I told him, "your name comes from the Bible, and the girl who gave you your name chose it because she hoped you would be blessed and would never be harmed again."

I leaned over and stroked the side of his neck, one of the few places on his body that was not scarred or infected or covered in sores. "I promise you that you will not be harmed again."

THREE:
SIMON AND BRYAN

It became clear that Simon would survive his wounds and troubles. For one thing, he was eating everything that wasn't nailed to the ground and many things that were. Within a few weeks of Simon's arrival on the farm, his coat began to grow back. He stood a bit more on his feet each day. He took his medicine and drank his water and ate his cookies and apples and was always watching the barn door, waiting for me to come through it with my treats and copy of *Platero and I.*

Simon loved life — I could see it in his eyes. He wanted to live, and I knew donkeys are hardy, among the most durable animals in the world. Under the proper care, he would recover unless there was something terribly wrong with him that we could not see.

He was almost instantly more comfortable. The lice were dead and the flies stayed out of the shadows of the hay feeder and the barn. His infected jaw healed; the swelling reduced. He was taking painkillers for his twisted feet, and he figured out how to chew without the teeth that had been removed.

His eyes were bright and clear, and always focused on me. I saw right away that Simon loved attention, and that he needed it. It was like breath to him; he just closed his eyes and purred when his soft nose and ears were rubbed.

Simon and I wandered through the beautiful town of Moguer. We stopped to visit the shy female burro Platero loved, and the little shepherd playing his pipe under the twinkling light of Venus. We sniffed the flowers in the church garden and watched the sparrows fly out of the vestry trees. We tasted the peaches Platero helped himself to from a neighbor's grove. We witnessed his encounters with children playing on the farms he trotted past.

Donkeys are known to love children, and they seemed to bring life to Simon, to stir his soul in a special way. I saw this with McKenzie Barrett, who named him. It was even more powerfully evident in his new friendship with Bryan, a twelve-year-old boy who lived up the hill.

When Maria and I first spotted the small trailer about a quarter mile up the hill from the farm, we just assumed no one was living there. Some of the windows were boarded up with plywood, much of the asbestos siding on the side of the house was cracked or broken, there were shingles missing on the roof, and brush grew over the front door. The mailbox had no lettering, and the hinge to the mailbox door was broken, so it dangled down toward the road. We never saw any lights on, nor was there smoke from the chimney. People often associate the country with beauty and industry, and cities with poverty, but there is a kind of grinding, soul-shattering poverty you see off the main roads in upstate New York and other rural areas that is heartbreaking.

In the country, poor people and families are up against the elements in a very direct way, and it is never more wrenching than in the middle of a brutal winter when they struggle to stay warm. A neighbor shocked us by telling us that five people lived in that trailer: a mother and her four children. The husband had been taken out by the state police and ordered by a judge not to come within a thousand yards of their home.

Shirley was struggling, and everyone on the road contributed some firewood and soup and clothes if they could. We signed up. The oldest boy, Bryan, we were told, went up and down the road looking for work. He was a nice kid, a bright kid, and people found odd jobs for him. Our neighbors told us to look out for him.

We didn't have too long to wait to meet Bryan. One bitter cold afternoon, I went outside to feed the animals. A freezing rain was falling; the road was slick and the wind merciless. My eyes were tearing up just from being outside. I was heading out to feed Simon in the barn when my dog Rose froze, turned, and growled. The hair on her back went up and she moved toward the bottom of the driveway. She was focused on the big maple tree, where a number of rabid skunks had emerged previously. I was about to turn back to the farmhouse to get my .22 — they had to be shot quickly — when I saw a pair of sneakers and skinny bare white legs sticking out from the base of the tree.

I was alarmed, as I couldn't imagine any good scenario where a pair of exposed young legs would be lying still by the road. I ran toward the tree and as I did, I saw a young boy — dressed in a nylon windbreaker, shorts, and sneakers — jump up, wave, and run off up the road.

I yelled after him to stop and that I wanted

to talk to him, but he just kept going, up the hill and out of sight.

What was he doing dressed for summer on such a cold day? What was he doing lying in the shadow of my maple tree?

I saw him several times in the next few days. I knew he lived in the trailer up the hill; I couldn't imagine where else he might have come from.

One afternoon, I looked out of my study window and I saw him at the rear pasture gate. Simon had walked over to him, and the two were standing head-to-head across the pasture fence. I ran outside, and when the boy saw me he started to move away.

"Wait," I said. "You don't have to run off. I've seen you around the farmhouse. Tell me what you're doing here. Can you tell me your name?"

The boy seemed to size me up. He was good-looking, thin, tall with a shock of brown hair. His eyes met mine and he held the gaze. "I'm Bryan," he said. "I'm sorry, but I've been here for your Wi-Fi." Bryan reached into his pocket and took out an iPod. His grandfather had given it to him for Christmas, he said. His grandfather lived in North Carolina, and Bryan had not met him yet, but he sent a present every Christmas. This year it was an iPod, and Bryan

65

loved it, it was cool, but his grandfather didn't know that they didn't have Internet and he couldn't download any music. He saw my satellite dish, he said, and so he had been hiding across the street and behind the tree.

Why, I asked, was he hiding?

"My mom says taking somebody else's Wi-Fi is like stealing," he said. "I'm sorry. I haven't been able to listen to any music, it's making me crazy." Bryan apologized again, and offered to do some chores in exchange for the Wi-Fi.

I said he was welcome to use the Wi-Fi anytime; it didn't cost me anything extra to share it with him. I had enough, I said. Would he be interested in coming into the house where it was warmer? He could call his mother and ask permission. I knew his mother; she came by often when she couldn't find her dog. I knew the dog as well. He was tethered to a tree behind the trailer all day and many nights, even in rain and snow. Sometimes he would break away or chew his way through the tether and run down the road. Maria and I would often bring him back.

In the country, interactions between kids and adults are not as uptight and wary as they tend to be in the city and suburbs. I never would have invited a young boy into my home when I lived in New Jersey, but here, neighbors take care of neighbors, and if kids are late for the school bus or their parents forget to pick them up — it happens — they come by and ask for help. You give it.

Bryan didn't want to come into the house, though, and I didn't push. He said he wore shorts all year, and he didn't need or want a winter jacket. I didn't push that, either. But I didn't want him lying around freezing outside in his shorts. So we compromised. He could come into any of the barns where it was warmer anytime he wished and visit iTunes as often as he wanted. I kind of liked the idea. A new use for the venerable and wonderful barns.

I asked him if he had seen the donkey, and he said yes. He asked me his name and I told him Simon's story. I was surprised to see tears coming down his face.

"I have an idea," I said. "Simon could use some visitors, and he loves kids. How about if you brush him every morning in exchange for the Wi-Fi?" There were sores and rough spots, I said, but it would be nice to brush his forehead and neck and parts of his back.

Bryan lit up at the idea, and I took him back to the barn. We grabbed a brush and I opened up the back barn door. Simon was standing under the feeder. I noticed he was standing more. His legs were getting stronger, and his balance was returning.

I showed Bryan how to check Simon's wounds, and told him to keep away from the sores and the blackened skin. Then I stepped back. Simon looked at me and then he pricked up his ears and turned to the boy. He seemed excited to see him, almost as if he recognized him. He uttered a soft bray — a whisper, really, as he didn't have his voice back yet. I wondered if he was thinking of the boy at his old farm, the one I knew had fed him.

I asked Bryan if he was familiar with donkeys; he said no, this was the first one he had ever seen. He was completely at ease. Country kids are not cloistered in the way city kids are. They see animals all around them and often approach them. I suspected Bryan had done a lot of roaming in his life and was comfortable with all kinds of animals.

Donkeys pick up on things like that. I had noticed they get skittish around city people and their kids who approach them fearfully and carefully. They sense their unease immediately and often get wary themselves. Simon liked Bryan and understood he was a friend, and perhaps he sensed the boy could use some healing, too.

Every morning after I visited and fed him I saw Simon look up the road for Bryan, who would pass by on the way to the school bus stop. Bryan usually ran up to the gate on his way down the hill and called out to Simon — sometimes he had a piece of apple for him. In the afternoon, Bryan would come up the hill, walk up the driveway, and wave to me in my studio. He would unlock the gate, walk through the barn, and come out the other side into Simon's pasture.

Bryan would take out his iPod, go to iTunes, and download some music — I got him an iTunes gift card as an advance on his work with Simon — and while the music was downloading, he would talk to Simon, brushing him carefully. Simon listened attentively, looking at Bryan as if he were soaking up every word. Donkey lore is filled with stories of the love donkeys and children have for one another. In the Kabbalah, an old rabbi explains that God made donkeys the guardians of children, because children are pure and filled with love and emotion, not yet tainted and corrupted and made angry as their parents often are. The rabbi says that donkeys are sacred messengers of God, and that children and donkeys talk to one another.

I saw that happening on my farm. Bryan, like most boys his age, was not comfortable talking. He told me that his mother had told him that I was famous and that he was not to bother me. He was never really at ease around me, although we came to like and respect each other.

As I sat across the driveway in my studio, though, I could hear a steady chatter — Bryan could hardly stop talking to Simon, and when I looked up, I saw the two of them head-to-head, conspirators in some ritual I was not invited to be a part of. I came to love seeing Bryan and Simon together. Sometimes, Bryan would invite his brothers and sisters to come and say hello, but they were too shy and clearly uninterested.

I could see that Simon connected with the needy, perhaps broken, parts of people. When I came out to say hello to Bryan one afternoon, I paused at the barn door, not wanting to intrude on the conversation I could hear, but also curious.

Bryan seemed to be telling Simon about his father. There was a restraining order out against him, he said. He had fired off a rifle one night when he was drunk and he was not allowed to visit. He missed him, Bryan told Simon. They were supposed to go hunting together, but now it looked like it would never happen.

Bryan told Simon about school, about the soccer team, and about an English teacher he hated and who hated him.

Simon seemed to be snorting in response; he was listening carefully. It is all too easy to project our thoughts onto an animal, but he looked sympathetic — it's the only word I can think of to describe Simon's demeanor. And if Bryan perceived him that way, then what a gift to them both. I knew that Bryan didn't want to share those stories with me, and I respected that. Animals are the world's best listeners. It's one reason so many people love them.

I opened the door and walked outside, and Simon brayed softly at me — his bray was just a squeak really. Bryan kept on brushing. He told me he had fifty songs on his iPod now, and he thanked me for the Wi-Fi. I wondered if Bryan would be leaving his job shortly, now that he had his music.

I needn't have worried. Every day for the next three months Bryan came by twice a day. Once when he was sick and home from school, he came down to see Simon in his bathrobe and pajamas, to talk to him and brush him.

Then one day Bryan didn't come. Simon waited for hours at the gate, but as it got dark, I think I knew he would not be coming again.

The next day I drove up the hill to the trailer. It was empty; the family had moved out. A "For Sale" sign was tacked to the door. I heard some barking and walked up to the side of the house, and I found the dog tethered to his tree, a quantity of kibble scattered across the ground, a filthy water bowl almost empty. Bryan's mother had left a note with my name on it.

She had met another man, she wrote, a good Christian man, and they had moved to a small town south of Albany. They would not be coming back. Thanks for being good to Bryan, she said, and would I say good-bye to Simon for him? He loved that donkey. Oh, and one more thing. Their new home didn't take dogs. Would I possibly take their dog onto the farm and care for him? Or if not, would I find him a good home?

The dog, a five-year-old golden retriever named Jake, was a mess. His fur was matted and he barked obsessively. I did find a home for Jake with a family down the road, but I heard later he got loose and was struck and killed by a car.

Simon never saw Bryan again, but every

afternoon he waited for him to come up the hill. Simon never forgot to look for him.

FOUR:
SIMON'S FIRST HOME

When Simon was removed from the place where he had suffered such neglect, the farmer had told the police that the donkey was not his — that he had taken him as a favor to someone who had sold him two horses and then dropped him off for just a short time. Simon was already in bad shape, the farmer claimed, and the donkey's condition wasn't really his fault.

I didn't know if the story was true or not. People often dropped donkeys off in trades, or unloaded them as part of some bartering arrangement. What made me consider it was Simon's obvious affection and trust for people, especially children. I was convinced that Simon had been some family's donkey, almost surely a farm family. Perhaps he had been a guard animal, protecting sheep. Perhaps he pulled firewood or kept a horse company. Maybe he was a child's donkey, and was ridden around a farm.

I decided to try to find out. The donkey came from Maplewood, Vermont, the police were told. Vermont is right next to the part of New York State where I live. I'd worked as a reporter in a number of major cities; I ought to be able to find a farm in Vermont.

I wasn't quite ready to see the farmer who was charged with neglect; his hearing was still some weeks away and I thought I ought to wait until that was over. Several people had warned me about contacting him, thinking it wasn't a good idea to approach him after his arrest.

I knew I would have to do it someday, though. I began to understand that Simon had triggered a journey, literal and figurative. I was curious, of course; I wanted to know about Simon, but I kept going back to the compassion thing, too. What was it? Why do some people have it and others don't? Why do we feel so much compassion for animals and so little compassion for people? Why was it sometimes so easy, sometimes so hard?

One morning, I drove to Maplewood, a small farming community about two hours from my farm. There was a coffee shop, a convenience store, and, down the road, a farm supply outlet. No one at the coffee shop or convenience store had any information that could help me with my search, but the owner of the farm supply told me there had been a farm down the road, one with donkeys, horses, and sheep, but the farm had been sold more than a year ago.

They had two donkeys, the man remembered. Nice people — had two kids, an older girl who lived in Boston, and a young boy whose name he couldn't recall. The name of the farmer was Jim Tunney. He thought he was a mechanic now, working for the John Deere dealership near Rutland. The Tunneys lived over in the next town now. Bad year for small farmers.

I had a feeling the Tunneys might be who I was looking for. I drove to the next town — a village, really. I asked around with little success, but lucked out in a small grocery store. I was told the Tunneys lived just behind the tiny town's shopping center.

I drove around, found the modest yellow split-level, and knocked on the door. I saw a small corral in the back with a pony inside. Two cats scurried away from the front of the house.

A woman answered the door; she seemed gracious and welcoming. I guessed her to be in her midforties. I told her who I was and why I was there. I heard someone playing a video game behind her in the living room and could see a boy about twelve behind her at a console.

I gave her the name of my website and told her she could check it out while I waited — something I used from time to time as a form of ID. She yelled to the boy, Sean, to come over. He shook my hand, and I asked him to look up www.bedlamfarm .com. I said I didn't know if they had owned the donkey that was now on my farm, but I warned them that the pictures might be disturbing.

Cindy then introduced herself, invited me in, and told the boy to wait a minute. Her husband, Jim, was at work, she said, and yes, they had once had a nearby farm. They had to sell it nearly a year ago, she said, and they had to sell their donkeys, too, which broke their hearts.

She then told me that they had had two donkeys on the farm, a female and a male named Aengus, spelled in the Irish way.

They were able to keep Sean's pony, but there was no room for the donkeys, no money. It was a hard thing, and I could see that from the sadness in her face. Sean was watching me intensely now. He asked his mother if he could look on my website and she nodded. The room was simply furnished but comfortable, a mix of old sofas and tables that I was sure had come from the farm and new things that seemed to fit the house more closely. I looked over at a coffee table next to the sofa — on it was a photo of two donkeys, side by side, a small, freckled-face female and a larger donkey with big ears and wide round brown eyes. It was Simon, no doubt.

"Oh, God," said Sean, looking at the photos on my website. "Mom, look at this." The two of them browsed through the photos, Cindy shaking her head, the boy looking as if he were about to cry. He didn't. I told them the story. I said I hadn't come to upset them; I was just looking for Simon's story.

Cindy told me how the farm had gone under. They couldn't make the bank payments any longer or buy feed. They decided to keep the pony — it was manageable — but they had to find a home for their two horses, two donkeys, and twelve dairy cows. They sold the cows to a neighbor. The female donkey went to a farm near Montpelier; Cindy said she knew that was a good home. The new owners wanted to breed her, and she was fine there. Jim had found a buyer online for the horses and the other donkey. The buyer had a farm in New York State. It was a hard time, she said. They couldn't afford to ask too many questions.

Jim hadn't liked the man in New York much, but he traded in equines and said he would find a good home for the animals and take a cut from the sale. He was a trader, really, as well as a farmer. Jim said it was the best deal they could get, and they didn't have a lot of choice. Simon was part of the deal. The buyer had told Jim that he was confident Simon would end up at another farm.

Cindy and Sean were shocked and shaken. I knew how hard it was to find another home for an animal you cared about; you always worried about how they were doing. It seemed a leap of faith under the best of circumstances, and I understood that Jim had done the best he could under the worst of circumstances. There aren't a lot of places to send an animal like a donkey, especially not in hard times, when people were abandoning donkeys and other animals all over the country.

They peppered me with questions about Simon — how was he doing, how much space did I have? They asked if they could come and see him; they were so grateful he was at my farm. They wondered what had become of the horses.

Cindy told me that Simon had come to

their farm a couple of years before Sean was born. They had bought him for their daughter, who was now a web designer in Boston, but he had become Sean's donkey. He had been named for her grandfather, who emigrated from Ireland. The whole family loved Aengus; he used to bray at them all day from his pasture right behind the house.

Sean had ridden Aengus when he was little, and they walked all over the farm together. Sometimes, in the summer, said Sean, he would sleep out in the barn with Aengus and then they would walk out in the woods behind the farmhouse. Aengus was good on a halter, he said. He loved to walk around the woods, nibbling on leaves and underbrush.

Cindy made me a cup of tea, and I told them about our plans for Simon, our commitment to healing him. I didn't want to stay too long. I imagined this wasn't pleasant for them.

Cindy's eyes were moist as she walked me to the door. Sean, quiet, had gone back to his video game. "He and that donkey were together their whole lives," she said. "It was just awful when the trailer came for Aengus. Sean said he wanted to be there, so we agreed. Maybe that was a mistake. It was awful, Aengus — Simon — just bucked and kicked and screamed when we put him on the trailer. He knew what was happening, and Sean just stood there hugging him and crying. What could we do? We couldn't afford to feed him and we weren't going to starve him." Maybe, she said, it would be good for Sean to see him again. She'd talk to Jim about it. Maybe it would be upsetting for both of them. It was, she said, the toughest thing she ever had to do. Aengus was like a member of the family; he did everything but come into the house for dinner. They all loved him.

She thanked me for coming. They would follow Simon's progress on the website. She took my number and said they would call me about a visit. She said I should call if there was anything they could do.

I said my good-byes. Sometimes, I just know I will not see certain people again, and that was the case with Cindy and Sean. As much as they loved him, I didn't think they could bear to have Simon in their lives anymore. He was in the past for them, and they knew he was all right now.

It was an important trip for me. It broke my heart to imagine the wrench for Simon and this family when they had to give up their farm and let him go. It also helped explain how loving and trusting Simon was, and why he loved children so much.

Beyond that, it showed me that some people had a boundary when it came to compassion, especially for animals. They loved having a donkey, they loved Simon, they hated to lose him. But that was a chapter in their lives. There was a point where they simply had had to let go; they had to take care of themselves and their own lives. That was a kind of compassion, too, a kind of perspective.

I saw that I needed to understand what had happened to Simon. I needed to put the whole story together, not really for him — he was in good hands now — but because there was something inside of me that I had to come to see and know.

It seemed that Simon's life bore out the drama of the donkey. Loved, worked, used, and discarded. He had endured and been reborn into another life.

■ ■ ■ ■

PART II
THE CALL TO LIFE

■ ■ ■ ■

FIVE:
THE CALL TO LIFE

Simon came to life in stages, slowly, unfurling like one of those slow-motion videos of buds opening in the spring. When I looked at him each morning, I couldn't see too much difference. If I looked at a photo or video from the previous week, though, his progress was astounding.

It is always miraculous to watch the way animals heal. They have no therapy, no machines, no expensive procedures, yet their bodies can heal themselves in the most astonishing ways.

Perhaps it is because they are not aware of their suffering. They don't know — as humans do — how bad off they are, how much they are struggling or hurting. They feel pain and discomfort, but they don't dwell there. For Simon, I always thought, pain was a feeling, just like feeling strong or well. A space to cross, something to accept and endure.

Donkeys are obsessively ritualistic. They do the same things in the same way every day. There were already two trails crisscrossing Simon's small corral, where he walked on the same path each day, and he could still barely walk at all. He made his rounds in the corral, to the bush on the right, the downed limb on the left, the grass on the other side.

This seemed to me a miraculous demonstration of his will to live and the healing power of the natural world. Just a few weeks earlier, we had considered putting him down as an act of compassion. Now, we could hardly wait to get out to the barn to see him get healthy. And mercy meant something different.

I still couldn't get the neglectful farmer out of my head. What was mercy for him? What was he owed? We could arrest him, trash him on the Internet, make him pay a $125 fine, but I was drawn to the murky questions that no one had answered.

What is a donkey's life worth to humans? Is it more than a traffic ticket? Less? Was there any good reason to neglect an animal like this? Any good excuse? If we owed Simon a better life, do we owe the farmer any consideration? Even to the extent of wondering what could have driven a man who lived with animals to such neglect?

As always with animal issues, I was reminded that Simon was not part of the discussion. The fate of almost all donkeys and many animals lies in human hands, and donkeys have been making their way in the world for a very long time. Simon didn't ask to go to his new farm, didn't ask to be rescued, didn't consent to be adopted by me.

Perhaps that's what makes our decisions about animals so intense, so laden, so filled with anger and conflict. The decisions are all ours. All Simon did was to heal, yet that was the most important thing.

Day by day, his eyes cleared, the cloudiness and infection moving out. He was able to see.

His ribs were not sticking out any longer, his stomach was beginning to fill out, and he did not look emaciated.

The fur on his blackened ears began to come in, as well as the fur on his shoulders and back.

The sores on his back healed.

The swelling in his jaw decreased, enabling him to chew normally.

His newly trimmed hooves gave him a solid footing, and he was walking with confidence again.

One morning in early summer I opened the back door, and I heard a loud and piercing sound echoing off the barns. It sounded like a trumpeting elephant. Rose barked and I froze.

I looked over to the pasture, and there was Simon, standing by his hay feeder, his big head sticking out, his ears back, releasing a window-shattering bray at the sight of me.

It was a beautiful sound. I ran back into the house and grabbed my video camera. He was still going by the time I returned. Clearly, his throat and lungs had recovered. His bray was not exactly musical — it was loud and up and down, back and forth, full of wheezes, coughs, and off-key notes.

Maria came running out. Simon was still braying, and she and I broke into applause. I put the first video up on YouTube, and people loved it. After a few brays, I told Maria "It's the call to life," and I started posting it in the mornings, to start my day. Simon's bray became an affirmation, for me and for many other people.

There was something both joyous and defiant about the sound. This battered creature who was just learning to walk again seemed to be reminding me to value life, to use my time well, to face adversity with strength and grace.

It seemed that Simon had won a mighty victory that day, and he was sharing it with me. It was hardly lyrical, but it was one of the most beautiful things I had ever heard. I sometimes cried when I heard it, though more often I laughed.

The day that Simon first brayed, I decided to go on a short walk with him, out of his small corral and into the larger pasture beyond. There was tall grass there, a couple of apple trees, fallen limbs, and brush that ran along the road. The pasture sloped up a hillside, and was perfect grazing ground for donkeys.

Lulu and Fanny were still in the smaller pasture behind the farmhouse. It was much too soon to put all three donkeys together. Simon was still too frail to risk getting kicked or chased. And Lulu and Fanny were the royalty of the farm — imperious, coddled, and entitled. We had been warned that Simon would get a skeptical reception from these two strong and powerful sisters. They had had a very different life from Simon's, bred on a well-run donkey farm, given fresh hay and cookies and shelter and pastures to roam every day of their lives.

After lunch, I put a couple of apples in my pocket and opened the gate to Simon's pasture. He was so much better, but his fur was still raggedy and he was shaky if the ground was uneven. The farrier said his legs would hurt for a long time, and we had to be careful not to overdo his exercise. I walked into the pasture and stopped to say hello to Simon — his ears were up and he was watching me closely.

I patted him on the shoulders, said good afternoon, and then walked over to the corral gate, opened it, and stood on the other side. I've learned something about how to communicate with donkeys, and there is no equivalent for donkeys of the "come" command that trained dogs love to respond to. In fact, there is no command at all that works for the donkeys I have known. They are agreeable creatures, but they do not like being told what to do, and if you show that you really want them to do something that doesn't involve food, you may be standing out in the sun for a long time.

The downfall of the donkey, his Achilles' heel, is curiosity. They are intelligent creatures, fascinated by every movement or sound. If you put a watering can in the pasture and it wasn't there the night before, each donkey will notice it immediately, approach it, and sniff it. They can't help it. They have to know what is going on. Carol taught me that the best trick to get donkeys to do something — the only trick that works — is to make them curious and they will come.

I didn't call to Simon to join me or give him anything like a command, or even look at him. I just took a carrot out of my pocket, started chewing on it, and walked a few feet out into the pasture, looking away. I must have shown too much eagerness, because Simon wasn't moving. He was looking at me, trying to figure out what I wanted. But he wasn't budging. The sun was getting warm, the flies were circling, and I was getting a bit restless. I do not have a fraction of the patience that donkeys do, but I am just as stubborn. We connect on that level.

Simon was chewing it over. I could see him looking at me. Every time I had seen him in the pasture, I had brought him food — hay, cookies, carrots, apples. He liked that arrangement and did not really see any reason to change the procedure. If he just stood there, I would probably eventually come to him. It was not his idea to take a walk into the pasture, so why do it?

There were two reasons, and I was confident both would work, if I stayed patient. One was the carrot he saw me chewing. He would have spotted the others sticking out of my pocket by now, and he wasn't about to sit around watching me eat his snacks. Secondly, he had not been out of his little corral, and before that, his confining pen, since he arrived at the farm. There was interesting stuff to see out in the big pasture — cars on the road, fallen tree limbs, acres of green grass, and who knows what else.

I stood there, checking my cell phone messages, eating my carrot, drifting farther out into the pasture. Sometimes that worked with Lulu and Fanny, sometimes not.

It took about four minutes. I was checking e-mail on my iPhone when I saw Simon trot down the slight incline through the gate. In a few seconds he was alongside of me. I gave him a carrot. I love the smell of the meadow, and Simon seemed to like it, too. The smell of fresh grass is sweet, and I am sure he was drawn to it. In the distance, the village of West Hebron twinkled in the sun.

Down in the valley, cows spread out over a pasture. A large tractor collecting the first-cut hay was behind them in another field. The blackflies had come out, but not the horseflies. Butterflies were making their little whirlpool circles all over the meadow, and overhead, I heard the lonely and piercing cry of a hawk circling for mice and rabbits. It is one of the loneliest sounds in the world, I told Simon, and one of the most beautiful.

Once again, I could not help talking to Simon. There is something about a donkey that is companionable, that will open you up, especially if the donkey is Simon, raised from the dead to live a fully appreciated life.

Simon chewed his carrot thoughtfully and took in his surroundings. He looked somewhat wistfully out into the other pasture, where Lulu and Fanny were standing still, watching. I see, I said. You are probably lonely, probably have been ever since you left your farm, your family, your child.

Of course he was. Donkeys are herd animals; they are never at ease being alone. They are often used to keep horses company and to guard sheep, but they need other donkeys in their lives. I had learned this from Carol.

Watching the news, it sometimes seems we live in a cold, angry, and violent world. If you have a rescue donkey who loves people, it seems like a warm and compassionate one.

My community — my friends, neighbors, blog and book readers — responded to Simon and his healing. I got letters from schoolkids, apples sent via UPS from Oregon, Facebook messages, e-mails, e-cards, flowers, bags of grain. I got blankets woven by donkey lovers. And visits from those in my immediate world. Simon touched people. There are rivers of compassion out there.

Simon and I began walking together regularly. It wasn't quite a straight line we followed — it never is with donkeys, even if you lead them by a halter. I explained butterflies to Simon; I waved to the UPS driver coming down the road to the farmhouse. I told Simon about how he delivered packages almost every day, and somehow I found myself explaining the Internet to him.

Scott, the UPS driver, honked and pulled over. I introduced him to Simon, and he waved. I would soon grow familiar with the sight of Simon over at the pasture gate, getting a carrot from Scott.

On one of our walks, Simon proved interested in several things: some nettles — painful weeds for humans to touch — were growing by the fence, and he went over to sniff them and eat a few. He was transfixed by a giant limb that had fallen off of a tree, and sniffed every inch of it for ten minutes. And he seemed drawn to a big old rotting tree stump sticking out of the ground. He paused a few times to tear up some grass and to chew it carefully and thoughtfully. His tail flicked away some blackflies. He seemed to want to stay beside me, but paid no attention to me. Simon gave the impression of loving life, of appreciating another shot at it. He always reacted to things as if he were seeing them for the first time. When he came up to a tree branch, he stared at it, sniffed it, nibbled on it as if it were the most miraculous thing in the world.

As we walked, I talked to Simon, speaking to him to encourage him to live and heal. It was more of a man-to-donkey thing, the age-old dialogue between strange men and asses. I explained that I was a writer. I told him about Lulu and Fanny. I told him the story of how Maria and I met. I told him I would be putting a halter on him soon, and we would be taking walks into the woods, and perhaps down the street into the town.

The morning of that first walk, I had brought Rose out into the pasture with me, and as we got out into the field, she came near. Simon put his ears down and charged at her. I yelled at her to get away — Simon could have stomped her into pulp in a second — and she ran off. I noticed that Simon did not like dogs, and dogs did not like him. Rose went back to the barn and stayed there.

Simon and I had gone about fifty yards on our walk that day. I had to be careful not to tire him. Also, if he refused to go back into his corral, I didn't really have a way of forcing him. Halters don't work well on donkeys if they don't want to move. They just stare at you while you pull.

I decided to be subtle. I turned around slowly and began walking in the opposite direction. Back to the corral. Once there, I would just put some grain in a can and Simon would come readily. I just didn't want him to get up on that hill, or to trot over to where the girls, Fanny and Lulu, were standing, still staring.

I walked back a few feet, touching the pocket where one carrot remained. Simon looked up at me, went off a few feet to explore some brush and nibble some leaves, and then turned slowly and started walking toward me.

There is a point with many animals — dogs, for sure, and, I believe, donkeys, too — where a strong attachment is formed, where you belong to one another, where there is a mutual sense of trust. Donkeys are intensely loyal and affectionate creatures in their own way. They love to serve and connect to their humans. And they are exquisitely sensitive. Simon and I had already been through a powerful bonding process — there are few ways to be more intimate than Simon and I had been these past few weeks as I was caring for him. He had decided to trust me, and I recognized as he followed me back to the corral that I wasn't really just tricking him. Sure, he wanted the carrot, but more than that, he wanted to be with me. I represented something to him: sustenance, affection, his new life.

When we got back to the corral, we had been gone about forty-five minutes. I closed the gate. Simon went to the water trough to drink some water. He and I gazed out at the rich valley below us — the view from Bedlam Farm is beautiful — and we saw the cattle vanishing in a fine mist as the temperature dropped and the wind came up. He snorted a bit, nuzzled me with his nose, permitted me to brush him, and then lay down suddenly, exhausted. This was where he would remain for the night, I imagined. He looked up at me as if he wanted me to sit down with him, and perhaps he did. I suspect it was lonely out there at night for a donkey. No donkeys, no people.

Good evening Simon, I said. Thanks for

the walk. Thanks for the company. I sat down next to him and broke the last carrot up into a few pieces. Tomorrow will be a big day for us, I said. I've seen you looking at Lulu and Fanny. I've seen them looking at you. Tomorrow, you will meet them. I will bring them in the far side of the barn, and put up a mesh gate between you and them.

I had seen the girls and Simon staring at one another, heard the soft braying back and forth. There was a sense of expectation in all three of them, as if they knew their lives were about to change.

You will get to know each other that way, I told Simon. You're not ready to be with them yet, but if things go well, perhaps in a couple of weeks you can join them and all be in the same field.

That night, I read Simon "The Sweetheart," from *Platero and I.*

The story is a sad one, recounting how Platero had to walk or ride past a burro he loves. She was behind a fence and up on the hillside. Platero always wants to go and see her, but his master tells him regretfully that he has no choice but to oppose his loving instincts. Platero's fair beloved watches him pass, as sad as he, her black eyes filled with reproaches.

Unwillingly, Platero trots ahead, trying at every opportunity to turn back, his every step a heartbreak.

I had seen Simon stare longingly at the girls, far up in the other pasture, as if they were some distant thing in a faraway land, beyond his reach, beyond his life.

That will change soon, I said. They will soon be a part of your life. Donkeys are herd animals; they don't care to be alone. But anyone who knows donkeys also knows they are romantics. They are quick to fall in love. They have great big hearts.

Six:
Sweethearts

Early the next morning, we let Lulu and Fanny into the south side of the barn. Simon was out in the corral on the north side, and there was a large door with a ramp on his side. The middle of the barn had a wooden gate with wire mesh that could be swung shut. We used it to separate sheep or to lock up the donkeys before the farrier or the vet came.

Maria and I had talked to vets and farriers and donkey lovers about the acclimation process and were told more or less what we had guessed ourselves. Simon and the girls should not be thrown in together suddenly. They needed to get used to one another, to sniff each other and get everybody's smells straight. We planned to open up the side doors of the barn in the daytime and let the three of them check one another out as much as they wanted.

The barn permitted the three to be much

closer than simply looking at each other from their different pastures. When Simon was stronger and two or three weeks had gone by, we would put them all together.

We knew donkeys well, and we had talked to other people who understand equines. Horses and donkeys are not, as a rule, gentle to newcomers. There are days, even weeks, of biting, kicking, bumping, and edginess over food.

Simon was gelded, but he didn't know it, and when the girls were in heat — they had not been spayed — there would probably be some excitement. Donkey romance is not gracious or delicate — there are no roses or poems or walks in the parks. It is also common for donkeys to greet newcomers by turning and kicking them in the head.

Around ten A.M., we checked on Simon, gave him his meds, and then opened up the barn door. Lulu and Fanny were waiting at the gate, peering through the slats, their heads down. Simon walked quickly into the barn and then, eyes wide, walked up to the fence. The girls and Simon sniffed one another for the longest time. Lulu's ears went back, but Fanny's didn't. Simon stood preening near the gate. We came back a few hours later and they were all still where we had left them. In the late afternoon, everybody got hungry. Lulu and Fanny went back up the hill to their pasture, and Simon went out to his corral to graze. We closed up the barn, enough for that day.

In the evening, I came out for my final check on Simon. He was standing up on the rise behind the barn, looking up the hill. Lulu and Fanny were in the pole barn staring back.

I heard Fanny's soft bray, and then Simon's louder response.

Simon seemed different to me. He seemed more alive, more intense. His eyes had a sparkle and focus I hadn't seen before. His chest was puffed out a bit.

I was excited for him. A donkey's life was not complete without the presence of other donkeys. And Simon could use some romance in his life. I worried a bit about the girls. They had led picture-perfect lives to this point. They had been raised in a clean and beautiful barn by a knowledgeable breeder and had come to Bedlam Farm when they were both quite young. They had acres of pastures to roam, hills to climb, brush and rocks to stand on and explore. Every morning they came down for their treat; every afternoon they consented to be brushed.

They guarded the sheep faithfully and

tolerated the border collies chasing the sheep around. In the seven years that I had had Lulu and Fanny, no fox, coyote, or stray dog had entered our pasture or taken a sheep. And Maria and I had both spent countless hours sitting with them, brushing them, sharing donkey daydreams with them. As our friends often joked, it was a perfect arrangement for them — plenty of grass, no men.

It was in the natural order of things for them to be with a male, though, and natural enough for Simon. The sniffing at the gate went well, but we really couldn't know how it would go when all three were together.

I liked to think that Simon was getting his family back, both in donkey and human terms. But we had learned many times not to make any assumptions about what animals would do. There are plenty of animal experts around — lots of people who know for a fact what animals are thinking, what they will do. And there are even more animals around to demonstrate that they are unpredictable and unknowable. It is clear what they will do only when you see them do it.

Three weeks later, Simon was stronger. His coat was growing in, the blackened patches on his skin receding. His legs were a bit bowed and funky, but they were getting him around. He and I were taking daily walks around the pasture, and I soon hoped to graduate to the roads and the woods beyond the pasture gate. He was off all of his medications and free of the need for salves and ointments. The rest of his healing was in the hands of time and nature. There was no question he would survive; it was time for him to live a normal life. By now, I was posting the "Call to Life" videos up on the Internet several times a week, and many thousands of people started their day with Simon's bray.

It was a rare day he didn't have visitors. Simon was a ham. He loved a crowd and almost any kind of attention. It was time to take him out of his corral and out into the world. To live with the girls.

So early on a Sunday morning, we opened up the pasture gates. Simon looked up and then walked slowly up the gentle hill and through the open gate. Lulu and Fanny were up in the pole barn, staring down at him.

I noticed that he was moving toward them, but the girls were not rushing to him. Ken Norman, our farrier, had counseled us on Lulu and Fanny's attitude toward Simon.

It would be simple, he said. "We are the queens. He is just Simon." Ken was, as always, prescient.

Maria and I stood at the base of the pasture looking up as Simon approached the girls in the pole barn. He started toward Fanny, head down and sniffing. Fanny turned toward him, then slowly spun around. Without moving much, she kicked him squarely in the head with both hind feet. We could hear the thump all the way down the hill.

Donkeys use two tools when they challenge, attack, discipline, or fight — their teeth and their hind legs. They can easily kick right through a door. Once when a stray dog had crawled under the gate and entered the pasture headed toward the sheep, I saw Lulu charge the dog and grab his leg in her mouth. She flipped him about fifteen feet in the air, then turned as if to kick him. She didn't have to. He took off out of the pasture and down the hill.

Simon seemed startled by Fanny's kick, then shook his head, as if shaking off a horsefly. He moved toward her again, and she kicked him in the head again.

Then Lulu came up to Simon, turned around, and kicked him on the other side of his head. Simon stepped back a bit but didn't retreat. He didn't seem especially rattled. It was almost as if he had been expecting it. This, I was told, is a donkey's way of saying, "Hello, welcome to the farm."

It was not easy watching Simon get kicked in the head, and Lulu and Fanny each did it several times. This was their way of saying, "Okay, you can live here. We will put up with you, but don't get too friendly or too close."

As it happened, almost every one of Simon's mornings began with his getting kicked in the head by Lulu or Fanny, or both, and after a few months, it just became part of the farm routine.

Having ministered to Simon's many needs for months, and watching him struggle just to stand up, Maria and I found this kicking ritual hard to witness. In fact, it was almost impossible.

For a few days, we stood at the middle gate with apples and lured Simon back into his corral, just in case he needed some respite from his new barn mates. He didn't, really. This was another human projection — another faulty human perspective on the animal world. From the first, Simon wanted only to be with Lulu and Fanny, and after a few nervous days, we did what we always tried to do: we let them work it out.

SEVEN:
THE THEATER OF CHANCE

I was walking Simon down toward the path one afternoon when a minivan pulled past and slowed. A woman rolled her window down and looked at Simon, and asked me "Is that a mule?" No, I said, mules are hybrids between horses and donkeys; this is a donkey.

"What does it do?" she asked. I was uncharacteristically at a loss. Simon gawked at her, hoping, as he often does with strangers, for a carrot or an apple, or even a scratch on his nose. His ears went straight up at her high-pitched voice, his eyes wide.

It goes on walks with me, I said. Disappointed and puzzled, she rolled up her window and drove off. "You are a ghost," I said to Simon, "a myth, you don't really exist for most people in America."

What does it do? I kept wondering what a good answer might have been. A good question, it requires a thoughtful answer. A few years earlier, I might well have asked it myself.

We kept on walking, the donkey and the wanderer, two of the oldest clichés in the world. *This* is what he does, I thought. This is what donkeys have always done.

I can't blame people for not knowing much about donkeys. Why would they? It is a commentary on our time that few people have ever seen a donkey walking around, as they do in so much of the world and have for so many thousands of years. We don't love our history; we are too busy coping with now.

Simon's ancient ancestor is the African wild ass, *Equus africanus asinus;* the *"Equus"* signaling that donkeys belong to the horse family. Domesticated in Egypt or Mesopotamia circa 3,000 B.C., they've been working animals ever since. A male donkey is called a jack; a female is a jenny, and today there are more than forty million donkeys worldwide.

In their book *Donkey: The Mystique of Equus Asinus,* authors Michael Tobias and Jane Morrison point out that artists have long viewed donkeys as "spiritual companions in an ethereal realm of life and death; the donkey equals man in the theater of chance and is equally a part of that divine force in the universe." The idea of this equality, this partnership, speaks to the very particular place donkeys have held in our imagination. "The theater of chance" is an apt term for the donkey's dramatic, arduous, and adventurous journeys with men. The theater of chance is nothing more or less than life itself, erratic and unpredictable, filled with love, hope, opportunity, disaster, illness, war, and uncertainty. Every day, we enter the theater. Every day we learn what is in store for us.

There are many representations of donkeys in our collective cultural history, but few set the tone more than the legend of Jesus Christ and his small and ungainly donkey. How much of the story is true? Jesus was known to ride a donkey on his travels through the Holy Land, but as for the rest, I have no way of knowing. I do know that this legend changed the lives of donkeys for all time.

The story of Jesus and his donkey is perhaps the first recorded rescue of an animal by a human. Thousands of years old, passed down largely by word of mouth, the story has shaped some of our deepest feelings about the care of animals, and created a template for the bond between animals and humans that still exists today.

A poor farmer outside of the city of Jerusalem owned a sickly donkey too weak and small to do much work at all. Few farmers could afford to keep animals that do not work for them or earn money. Over time, he grew increasingly angry at his donkey, telling his family he couldn't afford to feed such a worthless creature, as the donkey could do him no good at all and was not worth the feed it took to keep him alive. He was thinking of killing him, he announced.

His children, who dearly loved the little donkey, begged their father to keep the donkey alive. But the farmer held his ground. "It's wrong," he told his children, "to sell an animal that can't do a good day's work."

The farmer's oldest daughter came up with a suggestion. "Father," she said, "let's tie the donkey to a tree on the road to town, and say that whoever wants him can take him for nothing." The farmer agreed. The next morning, he walked the little donkey out to the road in front of their home and tied him to a tree. He could not, he said, imagine anyone wanting to take such a worthless animal, even for free.

Many people passed the little donkey and walked away. It seemed as if no one wanted him. Then two young men appeared. They looked at the donkey and, without hesitation, asked if they could have him. The farmer, an honest man, told them the truth: "He can carry almost nothing," he warned.

"Jesus of Nazareth has need of it," replied one of the men. The farmer had heard of Jesus, the great teacher, and he could not imagine what need of the donkey he might have, but with relief, he turned the animal over to the two men.

They took the donkey to Jesus, who stroked the grateful animal's face and then mounted it and rode away. So it was that on the day we call Palm Sunday, Jesus led his followers into the city of Jerusalem riding on the back of a small, quite ordinary little donkey.

The donkey loved his master and devoted himself to him, carrying him everywhere, following him everywhere he went, even to Calvary.

When Jesus was nailed to the cross, the legend goes, the donkey repeatedly tried to approach him, as if to carry him away to safety. At the sight of his master crying out in agony, the donkey brayed and rushed toward him, but was brutally beaten back by soldiers and by people in the cheering crowd.

The donkey was poked and prodded by spears and swords and pelted with stones and rocks. Grief-stricken at the sight of Jesus on the cross, the donkey tried again and again to come closer, but was driven back each time.

The donkey turned away and hid in a nearby alley but would not leave. It was then, says the legend, that the shadow of the cross fell upon the shoulders and back of the donkey, and there it stayed for all time, imprinted on the backs of donkeys to this day.

It is this story that seems to have first cast the donkey as the spiritual and long-suffering companion of human beings.

Today, donkeys continue to labor, often thanklessly, on behalf of humans. They come in all shapes and sizes, and several different colors. They live in deserts, on mountaintops, in villages and on farms. While the classic image of the donkey in Renaissance paintings is sacred and powerful, the modern image of the donkey is less lofty. When we see images of donkeys at all, they are generally hauling freight around some overcrowded village.

The relatively few donkeys that live in

America are either working as guard animals, protecting sheep and alpacas, or living as pets of "gentlemen farmers," often keeping high-strung horses company.

Donkeys have a great reputation for stubbornness, but it seems to me this trait is misunderstood. Donkeys may owe their survival to their willfulness; they are believed to have a stronger prey drive than horses and a weaker connection with man. It is difficult, if not impossible, to force or frighten a donkey into doing something it perceives to be dangerous for whatever reason.

Some of this resistance can be eased or even eradicated by trust. Once a donkey gets to know and trust a human, it will often go along with reasonable requests. They are curious and eager to learn, but they seem to have seen enough of humans to be cautious around them. This is something many struggling species have not figured out, and it has probably saved many donkey lives.

I'm drawn to the Tao of the donkey, their inner and dominating spirit. There is something mystical about them. They are loyal, affectionate, intuitive, hardy, patient, stubborn. They are also unique among domesticated animals in that they work and live closely with humans, and become powerfully attached to them, but they never turn themselves completely over to us. There is a part of them that is beyond us, that they won't surrender, a kind of dignity and independent spirit that most domestic pets have lost in order to survive.

There is no other animal I can think of that has been awarded such a spiritual aura by human beings. Donkeys are not just tied to Christianity; the donkey is also frequently portrayed as a loyal, wise, and enduring animal in the history of Judaism, in both the Old Testament and in the Kabbalah, the journals of the Hebrew mystics.

In the Kabbalah, donkeys are the wisest of living things; they often appear carrying prophets and mystics who challenged bewildered rabbis about the teachings of God. Often, the donkeys are overworked or mistreated and neglected by their masters, but they are important symbols of faith, suffering, wisdom, and commerce. Whenever they appear, ideas are exchanged; wise men and prophets are on the move. Donkeys are often used as stand-ins for the poor and unfortunate in the Kabbalah, and God and his prophets and angels are always exhorting people to treat them well.

Artists as diverse as Shakespeare, Chagall, and Orwell have all been drawn to the symbolism of the donkey and featured the animal in their work. Donkeys have been portrayed in famous paintings carrying Hannibal, Napoléon, and Queen Victoria on their backs. A donkey is the subject of the only novel in Latin that has survived complete from the era of the Roman empire. *Asinus Aureus* by Lucius Apuleius (born A.D. 124) features a protagonist who becomes a donkey and experiences the hardships and simple faith of that animal.

One of the most original literary works ever conceived, *The Life and Exploits of the Ingenious Gentleman Don Quixote de la Mancha* by Miguel de Cervantes Saavedra, is also a great work of donkey literature. Published in the early seventeenth century, *Don Quixote* features animals who take political or moral positions; their actions speak to their nobility, weaknesses, and strengths. Like humans, they are imperfect creatures filled with contradictions.

In Cervantes's work, animals are not background characters; they are significant protagonists. Two of the book's four central characters are equines: Don Quixote's old horse, Rocinante, and Sancho Panza's beloved donkey, Dapple.

Without Rocinante and Dapple, *Don Quixote* is hardly a book at all. In the globe-trotting satiric commentary, the two equine companions are mirrors of the men who ride them into every imaginable predicament and misadventure. From battling giants who assume the form of windmills, being beaten by liberated prisoners, and falling for one Dulcinea after another, to wandering through wild and inhospitable mountain ranges, Rocinante and Dapple get them through.

Dapple's donkey diaries are one of the most inventive creations in literature — a chronicle not only of Spain in the seventeenth century but also of human beings who reveal themselves to be the sum total of many lunacies, great dreams, lost loves, and weeping hearts. Dapple endures, loves, rises and falls, lives and dies with every twist of the human's fortunes. It is the donkey who defines the man who rides him.

This then, is the theater of chance: man turning himself over to the loyal animal, trusting him through unimaginable challenges, confiding in him as a trusted soul mate.

When Sancho Panza thinks he had lost Dapple, he falls apart, giving way to endless doleful lamentations. He knows he had been diminished and does not believe he can make the journey alone.

I relate to this deeply — the story of Sancho Panza and Dapple. I believe that Simon came to define at least a part of me, and to reflect other parts. We were bouncing off each other, and still do, each touching a part of the other.

And that is one of the most powerful things about donkeys for me. You can communicate with them, even without words. They understand many things. Simon knows precisely when to approach me for a cookie, or when to press his forehead against my chest to offer me comfort. Through him I saw that I was closed and needed to open up. Through him, I found a powerful way for a man to understand nurture, something I previously thought came more naturally to women.

Through Simon, I discovered the power of healing and of selflessness, and I came to acknowledge the extraordinarily pure and powerful way in which a man can love an animal. This ancient idea of humans and animals journeying together through life is real. I experienced it, and I feel it still when I go to the pasture and Simon comes over to greet me. I rub his soft nose and tell him the story of my day. We are bound together.

I watched for the woman in the minivan, the woman on the road. I suspected she might come back. When she did, I would flag her down and answer her question "What does it do?" Simon, I would tell her, teaches me the meaning of compassion. That is what he does.

EIGHT:
TWO ASSES ON THE ROAD

With Simon, there was this very curious feeling that kept returning, again and again. *We had met before. We were not strangers. We had done this before.* Everyone I knew kept telling me how amazing it was that I had met this donkey and brought him into my life. But it didn't feel amazing. It felt oddly normal and familiar.

I never really felt as if I was doing something new — meeting a strange animal or beginning a new experience. It felt as if we had been together many times, and far back, since the dawn of civilization.

I had all sorts of issues in my life with intimacy and connection, but I was learning some powerful lessons about both: The more you open to connection, the more you get. The more you believe you are worthy of connection, the more connection appears in your life.

Just a few years earlier, the notion that

Simon and I had a history, that we had met before, would have been laughable. But now, sitting with him in a pasture, I just knew it was true. And so, I believed, did he. Simon and I were in a dialogue. How else to explain the instant connection between this balding, middle-aged man, a writer, bookish and brooding, and this genial, determined, and social donkey? From the first encounter, I felt as if I could talk to Simon, and he to me.

For a long while, I didn't tell Maria that I was having conversations with Simon in my head, and when I finally did, she just laughed. Of course, she said. I knew it. I can see it. Good for you. Maria did not need to be opened up to new experience; she was well ahead of me. She talked to birds and cats and squirrels all of the time. They often suggested themes for the pot holders, quilts, and pillows she made as a fiber artist. And, she confessed, she had been talking to Lulu and Fanny for a while. I'd listen to Simon if I were you, she said.

A few months after he arrived, I decided to try a halter on Simon so that we could take longer walks. I carried an apple in my hand, and Simon came down from the pole barn to get it and see what was up. Lulu and Fanny stayed behind, watching. I knew

124

once they heard Simon crunching in the barn they would appear, and they did. I had never halter trained either one. It never occurred to me to take them for a walk, and one would not have gone without the other.

They both were so gentle that Ken Norman, our farrier, rarely used a halter with them. He just sat alongside them and trimmed their hooves, and they stood quietly while he did. Simon was not so gentle. When Ken came to do his hooves, he kicked and bucked and nearly put Ken and me through the barn wall. I smacked him on the nose and told him to knock it off, and he did. I wasn't sure how he would handle the halter.

I struggled a bit with the halter and had to call Maria to come out and help me get it on Simon so that it fit right. Simon had clearly worn halters before, though, as he took it comfortably and didn't even seem to notice it.

I was nervous. I wasn't sure what would happen outside of the confines of the pasture and its gate. What if Simon balked? Wouldn't return? Tried to run off? Got spooked by something on the road? He was a lot more powerful than me, and I was not sure I could control him. But there was no doubt we were going to try.

I checked the halter and walked to the gate. Lulu and Fanny were curious, watching, but of course if they thought I wanted them to come out of the gate, they wouldn't. And they didn't. They hung back a bit, perhaps anxious to see what the silly man was doing now.

I opened the gate, said "C'mon, Simon, let's take a walk," and he trotted outside of the gate beside me.

Suddenly, I heard this anxious and panicked braying from Lulu and Fanny. Each morning for weeks now, their day had begun by kicking Simon in the head, usually in tandem and often several times. But now that he was being led away, they were outraged. It was not their idea; it was not in their plan. The braying was loud and urgent, and Simon froze in the driveway.

But I had been with donkeys awhile, and I knew some tricks, too. My pockets were filled with oats and molasses donkey cookies. I stood still while Simon turned back to look at his braying companions. Lulu and Fanny were calling him back to them. They might kick him in the head every morning, but that didn't mean he could leave without permission.

Simon was uncertain. He stood still. I waited a few minutes and took a cookie out of my pocket. Simon waited a few more minutes, and then made a decision. He walked forward to get the cookie. The ladies could wait.

The braying went on for a few minutes, but then Lulu and Fanny quieted down and watched. I thought we'd be fine as long as they could see Simon. I wasn't sure what would happen when we made it past the driveway.

Simon chewed his cookie and studied the situation. I think he liked being with me; he had come willingly through the gate. Generally, donkeys did not like to walk straight distances unless trained to do so. Simon looked over to his left at a bank of grass, and to his right at some shrubs. He veered over to the right and pulled some leaves off of a tree.

I tugged on the halter a bit and he dug in. When donkeys dig in, there is no way short of using a tractor to move them. I had to give him time. I showed him the cookies in my pocket and started walking. He still dug in. I waited a few minutes until he got bored, and then he decided it was his idea to walk and he started walking.

We did this start-and-stop for a few minutes. I think Simon was just a bit confused and distracted by Lulu and Fanny's pleas.

But it seemed as if he picked up on the idea. He started moving, and we walked down the driveway, perhaps twenty feet. He seemed very responsive to my tugs on the halter. They were gentle but firm.

I heard a truck coming down the road and stood in front of Simon. To tell the truth, I was pretty proud of us, standing there like that. Even in the country, one rarely — if ever — saw a man walking a donkey. I was joining the ancient fraternity. Perhaps Simon knew it.

Once the pickup got closer I recognized it. It was my neighbor Carr's truck, a battered green Toyota, the bed invariably stuffed with feed or hay or rakes and shovels.

Carr has a farm over the hill in Cossayuna. He's a grizzled, ruddy-faced man in his sixties who periodically pulls over to give me some guff about my farm and the way I run it. From the first, Carr had been mystified by my presence on this ninety-acre farm. "How do you make your living?" he asked me one day. "I write about dogs and animals and rural life," I said. "Yeah," he said, "but how do you make your living?" We have this conversation once or twice a month, but Carr can't seem to process it.

During the last big winter snowstorm he came by and yelled out his window that he had been watching the news about the storm: "I never knew winter was dangerous till my wife got us a television!"

I could only imagine what he would make of this scene.

The truck rolled right up to us and slowed. Carr looked at Simon and then at me. He shook his head and smiled.

"Well, well," he said. "Two asses on the road."

I cracked up. It was a great line, and how true. I didn't know how Simon would react to a truck idling so close, but he just took in Carr, one old donkey recognizing another, I thought. As loving as Simon could be with kids, there was also a grumpy, idiosyncratic side to him. He had been around.

I told Carr Simon's story, and he got out to check the donkey's wounds, which were still impressive. Then, still shaking his head, he drove off. Carr was a farmer, a real one, and I doubt he could conceive of any reason why a sane person would have a large animal he had to feed that didn't produce anything and couldn't be sent to market for meat. But he had gotten used to my strange ways.

I knew I would hear more about this.

After Carr pulled off down the hill and it was quiet again, I decided to cross the road.

Now it was my turn to talk to Simon.

"Pal, this is a love walk," I said. "Let's go see Maria." Simon turned his head, and I was surprised to see an elderly woman walking up the hill.

My road is steep, and sometimes hikers and people out for their daily walks come up, but it is a hard walk and usually attracts only kids building up their stamina for school sports or regular hikers and power walkers. Few people made it too far, and none were nearly as old as this woman appeared to be.

"Simon," I said, "look at the woman. She is dressed very strangely. A shawl like my grandmother used to wear, a long skirt, dirty and muddy from dragging across the road. She's wearing sandals, like a gypsy. I wonder who she is."

Simon was staring at her, my dogs in the yard were barking, and I looked back to see that Lulu and Fanny were staring also. The woman had a long, thin walking stick that she leaned on for support, but her gait was firm and strong. Her face was wrinkled and leathery. I saw her gray-black hair was tied back in a long braid.

There were not many people in my town and I was certain I had never seen her before. As she got closer, I could see her smiling and she seemed to be walking right toward us. I had a feeling we were her destination, yet I had never seen anyone like her outside of New York or another large city. She was exotic. Her skirt was colorful, with all sorts of symbols and patterns on it, even as the hem was covered in dirt and dust. I imagined it was painful for her to be walking in those sandals. I didn't want to cross because then she would come up behind us, and I didn't want to be rude if she was coming to see us.

It took her a few minutes to get up to where we were, and the closer she got the more astonishing she was. When she came near, she smiled at me and turned to Simon. She spoke to him in Spanish, and her speech was filled with trills, laughs, explanations, and declarations. She shook my hand, and her skirt swirled and her beads, necklaces, and bracelets jangled. I hadn't seen a gypsy in a long while — not since I was a reporter writing about them — but this was clearly a gypsy, I had no doubt about it.

I looked far down the road and saw two more people coming up the hill, both of them much younger than this woman. They looked like teenagers. She said in halting English that they were her grandchildren, and they were coming to collect her.

They had told her there was a donkey on the hill, and she loved donkeys. She had had one when she was a child and she loved them more than anything. She reached into her pocket and took out a biscuit of some kind and put it in her open palm and handed it over to Simon.

He was mesmerized by her — animals always feel the emotion of people who are connected to them — and she kissed his nose, rubbed the side of his face, and scratched his neck, all the while loving him and speaking to him in her native tongue.

Long before the teenagers reached us, she threw up her hands with a sort of helpless resignation, turned, and rushed down the hill toward her huffing and puffing grandchildren, her sandals slapping on the dirt road, her skirts pulling up the dust.

Simon and I were both blown away by this visit, speechless and wide-eyed. His ears were tilting like radar towers, and he tugged at the halter, as if urging me to follow her.

"I think she is a gypsy, Simon," I said. "A donkey lover." The woman turned at the base of the hill, waved, and blew us some kisses. I wasn't sure she was real, but I saw the tracks on the road, and Simon was still chomping on the hard biscuit she had given him. The three of them vanished down the curve in the road.

"This is already an adventure," I said.

Simon started to cross the road, and then, of course, stopped right in the middle. Since cars and trucks came down the hill at reckless speeds, this made me uncomfortable, but I knew he wouldn't stay there long, as there was tall fresh grass right on the other side.

Simon figured this out for himself and then walked across the road and started pulling the grass out. This set off another round of anxious — perhaps jealous — braying from Lulu and Fanny.

Simon was having none of that; he was beginning to enjoy his walk. So far so good. A lady with a biscuit who loved him, a man in a truck, fresh grass, cookies from me.

Donkeys are innately curious, and Simon always seemed fascinated by the world around him. Perhaps because of his lonely confinement, the world seemed compelling to him. He seemed interested in every truck, every kid, every person that he met. And this idea of exploring new territory seemed to please him.

I let him chew on the grass a bit, and then I said, "Come on, Simon, let's go see Maria. She is in her studio." I explained Maria's work to him, how she made fiber art

— quilts, scarves, pot holders, hanging pieces — and sold them on the Internet.

I loved this idea of explaining the world to Simon. It opened up a rich and deep vein in me. I was not the least bit self-conscious or uncomfortable with it. It seemed one of the most natural things I had done.

I do not talk to my dogs in this way, or other animals. I do talk to donkeys a bit, but especially Simon. I was beginning to understand why strange men — Jesus, Cervantes, Napoléon, Caesar, the pharaoh Ramses — had been talking to donkeys for centuries.

Something about the animals invited it, their companionability, their daydreaming, their spirituality, their curiosity.

We walked up the hill and appeared in front of the large plate glass window that formed the east side of Maria's studio. I tapped on the glass. Maria, bent over her sewing machine, broke into a wide grin. Frieda, her Rottweiler-shepherd mix, started barking, but Simon paid her no mind. He was not impressed with the posturing of dogs. He had seen too much, and I suspect he considered dogs a vastly inferior life form.

Maria came running out the side door. "Simon!" she exclaimed, and she brought a handful of dog biscuits, which he happily devoured. We were beginning to see that he was a garbage disposal. He ate anything: leftover vegetables, pasta, bread, and crusts. And dog biscuits. Why not?

We stood by the side of the road for a few minutes, all of us beaming. I was proud of the walk; Maria was delighted by the visit. So was Simon. We hung around for a bit, and then we turned around. Lulu and Fanny were beside themselves now. We were beginning to drift out of sight, and Simon answered them with a raucous bray. He seemed to have gotten some new marching orders, as he trotted rapidly — to my relief — across the road and back up to the pasture gate.

I patted Simon. I opened the trash can filled with supplies and took out three hard oat cookies. I gave them to him one at a time, and he chewed each one thoughtfully, carefully, thoroughly. I encouraged him with some praise and some gratitude. The evening sun was settling in among the gray-crystal rain clouds, and a soft breeze was tiptoeing up the valley. I scratched behind Simon's filthy ears, the gnats and horseflies scattering in panic, and I felt the dawn of joy between us.

Our work had brought us out into the

world, defined our relationship, suggested our future. We looked out at the town together.

Have I told you, Simon, that the soul of our world is money? It is all people talk about, all they care about. Who has time in this world to walk with a donkey, get to know one, or care about them? We are too busy making decisions, saving money, worrying about our future. Platero's world is gone, I said. I don't know if it exists anywhere in the world anymore.

Perhaps we can re-create a slice of it here, in this small hamlet in upstate New York, far from the crowds that make the decisions that run the world. The walk felt like that, it felt good, something powerful and old, something men and donkeys used to take the time to do. Let's do it again, Simon, I said. Let's try it while we can.

Simon was listening to me, his ears whirling to catch every tone in my voice, every emotion. He snorted, checked my hands and pockets, and walked to the pasture gate.

I dropped the halter, opened the gate, and walked him in. I took the halter off, and he and the ladies went running up the hill to the pole barn.

Two asses on the road. Just right.

NINE:
FOX ATTACK

As Simon grew stronger and healthier, he changed. He was, if anything, even more affectionate. But he also developed a bit of a swagger, a sense that he was the prince of the pasture — not one of the herd, but the leader of the herd. It was often necessary for Lulu or Fanny to kick him in the head, but it didn't seem to slow him down or humble him in any way.

He stood up on the hill with his chest puffed out — though his legs were still a little wobbly — and it seemed that this was his farm, his pasture. This former creature of deprivation had become the donkey of entitlement, perhaps because he was being spoiled rotten daily.

There was a tangible point, though, when Simon left the whole rescue thing behind — animals never have as much use for it as people do — and asserted his natural self, which was anything but cowed or piteous.

This was during the great Fox Attack of 2012, when Simon embraced his potential and cemented his leadership of his new farm.

We had a few chickens, including two Rhode Island Reds named Fran and Meg. I was taking a photo of one of our hens who was pecking at the grass about ten feet in front of me when I was startled to look in the viewfinder of my camera and see nothing but feathers trailing down from the sky. I looked up and the chicken was gone, just a pile of feathers left on the ground.

I looked all around but saw nothing. It seemed a hawk — we had seen her circling for days — had swooped down right in front of me and scooped our hen up and took her off for dinner.

We kept the hens in a relatively secure part of the barn. Other than the hawk, we had had no trouble from predators. We always credit the donkeys with keeping coyotes and stray dogs away; they are guard animals, protective of their pastures and the things in them. We had never had a run-in with a fox, but we had heard a lot about them from farmers. They are one of the smartest animals in the world: brave, stealthy, and intuitive. They seem to adopt strategies, stay away from humans, watch and wait.

The first sign of trouble came when I got up one morning to let the dogs out early. Frieda, our Rottweiler-shepherd mix, started barking furiously, and our Lab, Lenore, a peaceful creature, even chimed in. I ran to the front door and saw a neighbor walking with her husky and pointing up to the pasture.

Something was up. I ran outside and looked up the hill just in time to see Simon with his head lowered charging down the hill from the pole barn. I looked to the right and saw a bright red fox holding Fran in his mouth and trying to run up the hill with her. The fox looked up to see Simon charging straight at him. He sized up the situation, dropped the hen, and took off underneath the pasture fence where there was a small drainage ditch, the one place Simon could not pursue him. Then he vanished up the hill. Fran wobbled down to the barn and collapsed. She had deep bite marks on her leg and one wing.

Simon stood staring up the hill, snorting and breathing heavily as he watched the fox retreat. I ran over to the neighbor, and she told me what had happened.

She was walking up the hill with her husky when she saw Simon circling and then charging. She saw that a fox was pursuing one of our hens, Meg, who had run for her life, squeezing under the pasture gate and running across the road, where she was presumably still hiding in the tall grass.

The fox turned back and tried to grab a second hen — there was no sign of her now — when I let Frieda out and she had charged to the gate. The fox stopped, checked Frieda out, and ran to the other side of the pasture, ignoring Simon and Frieda, and sneaking around to dart in and grab Fran, who was hiding under the hay feeder. He got her, but not before Simon saw him and charged again.

I thanked the neighbor and looked up at the top of the pasture. I was astonished to see the fox sitting at the upper pasture gate, staring down at the farm, looking for the hens he almost got to bring home.

I called my neighbor who lived at the top of the hill, and he said, oh yes, there was a fox den up there. Four or five kits and mom and dad out hunting. He couldn't bear to shoot at the foxes once he had seen the babies.

I could, at least at first. Nobody with a farm and chickens will look the other way when a fox comes around. I grabbed my .22 and ran up the hill. The fox stared at me. Halfway up, I lay down, sighted the rifle — he was right in my sights — and fired. The fox gave me a you've-got-to-be-kidding look and then just sauntered off.

I told Maria we were in for it. We had never been up against a wily fox before, and we had heard nothing but horror stories about their perseverance and intelligence.

We collected poor Fran — she was alive but just barely — and got her into the barn. Maria got out her creams and ointments, cleaned out her wounds, and put her in a dog crate. Chickens are not nice to their injured colleagues; they will peck them to death if they can get near them.

We tried to figure out what to do about the other hens and went to find the survivors. When chickens are attacked, they flee toward the nearest hiding places. They might hide for a day or so. Chickens have no natural defenses and can't fly away from their predators or run too fast. All they can do is go into shock. We were worried we wouldn't be able to find Meg, but Maria went across the road and called out to her, and she popped her head up in the grass and ran across the road to Maria like a scared schoolkid running for her mom.

Many people read about this on my blog and e-mailed me or posted messages on Facebook urging me to build a predator-proof shelter, but I had been on my farm too long and had learned too much for that. Predator-proof chicken shelters are expensive, and even then, never truly predator proof. We valued the idea of free-range chickens. We loved seeing them parade industriously around the farm.

Besides, we had some weapons to use against the fox that might make a difference: Lulu and Fanny, and now, it seemed, our latest hero, Simon.

I kept seeing the fox all day, walking back and forth at the top of the pasture, keeping his eyes on his potential dinner. I imagined he was eager to bring food back to his offspring. He was also on to me. Whenever I went outside of the house with the rifle, he vanished, and when I was gone, he reappeared. There are all kinds of predators in the country, but none as cunning and determined as a fox. Every farmer I knew told tales of being outsmarted and defeated by them. One farmer, a neighbor, told me to forget about the chickens: "He will figure out how to get them, and he's smart enough to take them right out from under your nose."

The next morning, Maria and I drove the ATV to the top of the pasture, and we found the fox's den. It actually looked right down on the farm, and the fox — his mate, too, perhaps — could look down the hill and see the chickens pecking around. We had locked them up for a few days, hoping the fox might get distracted by some fresh opportunities — rabbits or mice, maybe even a woodchuck — but that was unlikely. He had put his mouth on one hen and gotten some feathers from another. He wasn't going anywhere.

The den had two holes on either side of a hedge — foxes build escape tunnels. As we walked near the den, we saw three kits — baby foxes — come out and play with one another, wrestling and running in circles. I got some photos of them and put them up on my website. This is it, I said to Maria. I can't shoot any of these animals.

And it was true. I didn't have it in me to shoot the mother or father and leave starving babies, and I certainly didn't have the heart to kill the babies. Perhaps I don't have the heart of a true farmer, but I just couldn't do it. We would have to think of something else.

As we puzzled and fretted, it felt a bit like we were under siege. Poor Fran was a horrible mess. I wanted to shoot her and put her out of her misery, but Maria was determined to nurse her back to health.

We had greatly underestimated Simon. He seemed to take the fox attack personally. Lulu and Fanny would circle around if a stray dog or coyote came around, but they were gentle souls and had never charged an animal like Simon had.

And that was just the beginning. The animals didn't really need our help as it turned out. Simon instantly turned into our own secret service, taking the idea of a guard donkey to new heights.

In the mornings, before we let the chickens out, Simon would climb halfway up the hill and stare at the fox den. When the fox appeared to patrol on the ridge, Simon walked back and forth with him, stomping his foot, charging sometimes, and glowering. Meg stayed close to Simon. Every morning when Meg left the barn, Simon came over, and she hopped on his back, catching an escort to the hay feeder where the good bugs and worms were. Simon would let her jump on and then trotted up to the feeder where Meg jumped off. He then took up position between her and the ridge, where the red fox was still patrolling.

The Rhode Island Reds sometimes

jumped on the donkeys' backs to peck at bugs and fleas there, but Meg had taken it a step further — she was definitely using Simon as a shield, as a big brother. He rose to it.

For days, Simon kept watch on the ridge. Two or three times, I saw the fox crawl under the pasture gate and creep down the hill. He never got more than a few feet before Simon would spot him and start moving up the hill, ears and nose down. The fox might have been unimpressed by me, but he was taking Simon seriously. An angry charging donkey is not a pleasant thing.

The fox would back up, slip under the gate, and go hunt somewhere else for a while. We didn't expect this truce to continue, but after a week, the fox drama just ended.

The fox had disappeared. He never came back. We no longer saw him at the top of the pasture, and after a few days, the chickens and Simon all began to relax, to let their guard down. He's just waiting for this, I thought, but I was wrong.

Maria and I drove up the hill and saw that the den was empty. The family had moved away, perhaps to a new location where some vigilant donkey wasn't waiting for them. There had to be easier ways to eat than to get by Simon.

So our perspective on Simon changed. He seemed, as usual, quite pleased with himself, all puffed up and important. He was the big guy on the farm now, the protector, the chaser off of predators, our hero. I just about burst with pride. My man, I kept saying to him, my man. Bedlam Farm became a pastoral place again, donkeys grazing up the hill, chickens pecking around in the grass.

But it was clear that this was his farm now, and he took his role seriously. Like dogs, donkeys like to work, and if you don't find some for them, they will find their own — gnawing on barns and trees, chewing on tires, moving cans around and opening them.

Simon had a role. He was the guardian donkey of Bedlam Farm.

TEN:
THE FARMER

As Simon recovered and wove himself into the heart of the farm, I kept thinking about the farmer. I knew he'd been convicted of animal neglect and fined $125. But other than that, I knew nothing much about him.

A neighbor of the farmer's e-mailed me and asked if she could come by the farm to see Simon and meet me. She said it was important to her to see how he was now.

Three days later, Jeannie drove her battered old Toyota pickup into the driveway. I saw it was a farm truck — the straw, jugs, chains, and bits were unmistakable.

Jeannie looked like a horse lover to me — she had that tall, lean, and muscled look. I guessed her to be in her late thirties. Her handshake was strong, but I could tell she was anxious.

She said she had seen Simon when he first came to the farm five or six months before the raid. He was tied up by the barn, and then he just disappeared. She hadn't seen him since. She had grown up on a farm near Rochester, and had two donkeys and loved them dearly, and she had a feeling something was wrong. She never saw Simon working or grazing or being fed or brushed.

She had been worried about him, and she felt guilty that she hadn't called the police. When she saw them arrive with the trailer, she guessed he might be dead.

She looked around the farm, and then we went to the barn. Simon and Lulu and Fanny, all of whom had come to appreciate treat-bearing strangers, came down to check her out and sniff her pockets. Jeannie knew what she was doing. She asked permission, then reached into the pouch in her jacket — horse people always have those — and held out a cookie in an open palm to each donkey. She looked Simon over quickly and then smiled. "Good job," she said. "From what I hear, this is a lot different than he looked up there. . . ."

She tickled the side of Simon's nose, which donkeys love.

What was the farmer like? I asked. She shook her head at first, and then shrugged. Country people never like to talk about their neighbors, especially to strangers. Neighbors are important, and so is their goodwill.

Well, she said finally, he was a quiet man, not friendly, not hostile. If you needed some help, he was happy to provide it, but he never wanted to talk much, and she never saw much of the son or wife. There was to be no socializing, no visiting. She got that message and respected it. She had seen some horses around. She thought he must have been trading some or buying them. They were out in the pasture behind the house. They had a small pole barn for shelter and looked strong and healthy, she said.

She had noticed things deteriorating a bit around the farm; she guessed he was having a rough time. She said she always thought of him as a decent, hardworking man, but obviously she had been wrong about that. No decent man could have allowed an animal to suffer like that.

"They should have put him in jail," she said, quietly.

I nodded but didn't respond. After Jeannie left, I went out to the pasture to brush Simon and check on his legs. I kept thinking about what she had said.

Was that so? I hear that judgment often — the idea that people who mistreat animals ought to go to jail. I also hear people say they do not trust anyone who does not love an animal. That there is something wrong with people like that.

I didn't feel that way. I have good friends who are not drawn to animals, and they are good people. I think the love of animals has become a religion in America, a faith. If you look at the news, you sometimes see an angry and violent country, but if that is so, animals are its soft place, its merciful heartbeat.

The definition of mercy is "the compassionate or kindly forbearance shown toward an offender, an enemy, or other person in one's power." The definition of compassion is "a feeling of deep sympathy and sorrow for those who are afflicted by misfortune." Compassion is the strong desire to alleviate the suffering of another.

Wouldn't the farmer be entitled to some of both? Or had his treatment of Simon forfeited that right?

Mercy and compassion are deeply ingrained in the human relationship with animals. There are hundreds of thousands of people in the animal rescue movement, locating animals in need, transporting them around the country, rehoming and rehabilitating them. There are thousands of "no-kill" shelters all over the country where animals spend their lives being cared for and fed rather than euthanized.

In America, the Left and the Right agree on almost nothing, but they do agree when it comes to loving animals and treating them well. It is difficult to think of any single issue or movement that is so unquestioned and supported as the love and care of animals in need.

Yet there is no national rescue group for people — no consensus on how to help the poor or if they should be helped at all. Social service budgets have been slashed all over the country as Wall Street bonuses soar into the billions. I am not a political person. I just wonder at the contradiction, and how narrow the prism of mercy and compassion can be.

For me, compassion — like writing — comes from moving to the edge of my comfort zone. I know that people who profess to love animals seem to show little mercy to humans sometimes.

I've seen the mobs online raging about cruel humans and abused dogs. I was first introduced to the great numbers of people who attack human beings in the name of loving animals when I wrote *A Good Dog* about my decision to euthanize my border collie Orson after he bit three people.

Digital mobs rarely kill people, but I see little mercy and compassion in their swarming. There are thousands of pages on social media devoted to horror stories about people and animals, and the rage I sometimes see there is breathtaking.

Where did I stand in all of this? Animals have made me better every time I opened myself to them. Could I feel this way about people? Learn to be more patient, less judgmental?

I think I knew the minute I met Simon that I had to go and meet the farmer, see his farm, try to understand what had happened. My heart broke for Simon and what he had suffered, but he was also a mirror. In feeling for him I had to also feel for the man who had done this to him. They were not separate things; they were parts of the same thing. Simon and I and the farmer were all connected — part of the adventure of life, the theater of chance.

I suddenly saw that I could not possibly be compassionate toward Simon if I did not at least try to understand what had allowed this abuse to happen. If we can do this to animals, we can to it to others, and ultimately we are doing it to ourselves. Donkeys have always carried messages to human beings, from Jesus to the Kabbalah to Simon in my pasture. Simon was shaping — perhaps reshaping — my heart.

It was just not enough for me to condemn and judge and dismiss. That was not, to me, the path to being a fully realized human. I didn't want to run away from what the farmer had done. I wanted to run to it, to put myself in his shoes.

One warm July morning I drove out to the small town north of Albany where Simon had lived. I had seen the address in the paper when the farmer had appeared before the town court and been fined. Since the recession hit in 2008, animal control officers reported the growing problem of people who could no longer afford to take care of their animals — dogs and cats dumped on the roads or brought to shelters, farm animals without enough food or proper treatment of sickness and injuries.

Many small farms were going under, and as farmers struggled to stay afloat, they cut corners wherever they could. It wasn't, I was told by a farmer friend, a decision anyone felt good about; it was a process that devoured the human spirit. Quite often, these farms had been in one family for generations. No one wanted to be the one to break that legacy. No one wanted to let go.

I had been a reporter for a long time in big cities — Washington, Philadelphia, Boston, Atlantic City. I am not afraid to approach people who didn't want to talk to me, and I had learned how to talk to people, even when it wasn't comfortable.

Still, I was anxious. It could not have been easy for this man, having the state police come and haul his donkey away and charge him with neglect in front of all of his neighbors. He would not be happy to see me. He was unlikely to want to talk to me. But I was more curious than nervous. I wanted to see how I felt around the man. I loved Simon, and it was hard not to look at his awful suffering and not be angry.

It took an hour and a half to get to Simon's old farm. I could see it was not and had never been a dairy farm; it was a crop farm. There was one small red barn, no big cow barns, no silos, no broad and sweeping pastures.

There was an old farmhouse next to the barn, and I saw some rickety wooden corral fences, the kind used to contain horses. I saw three horses standing by the gate. They looked a little thin to me, but not alarmingly so.

A dirt roadway led out to some fields in the back — one cornfield and some hay fields. The farmhouse was raggedy, the white paint peeling off of the front, the shutters broken and cracked, gutters falling off of the roof. The old gardens by the front of the house were overgrown and looked as if they hadn't been tended in years.

I walked down the road away from the house to see if that gave me a better view of the pen in back where Simon was kept, and it did open up as I walked farther south.

I took out my binoculars, which I was carrying in my camera bag, and looked through a break in the pine trees that blocked the view from the front. I saw the pen right away. It looked like an old hog pen to me; the wire mesh fence was tall and looked sturdy. The wooden pallets — the only shelter Simon had — came up in a steeple about four feet off of the ground.

To get shade or protection from the rain, Simon would have had to lie down and stick his head under the pallets. No wonder his skin had been blackened by rain rot. Outside of the pallet shelter, there was room for him to stand up and turn around, but not much more. There was no grass in the pen, so his only food would have been the hay thrown to him. It was a death sentence, that pen, back out of sight of the farmhouse. The farmer didn't have to even look at Simon, and might have already thought him to be dead.

Simon could have been in the horse corral. There was obviously some hay around; there was plenty of brush and bark out behind the house, for that matter. Donkeys can eat a lot of things if they are hungry — even if they are not. In much of the world, this would have been their fare.

That pen was no place to put a healthy male donkey. It was a prison, a death trap, the equine equivalent of a concentration camp. And I remembered that this was the first thing I had thought of when I saw Simon — he was a concentration camp donkey.

I walked back to the car and put my camera bag in the back before walking to the house. Bringing it would have been provocative and foolish. The farmer might want to talk to me, but who knows how irate he would become if I took a picture of him.

I stopped to take a few breaths. I didn't want to be angry. I hadn't come to confront him, but to understand him.

I walked up to the front door and knocked. I heard some footsteps, and a thin, haggard-looking woman in her late forties opened the door. Only her head and her arm were visible. She looked as if she was not expecting good news or friendly visitors.

"Yes?" she asked without any hint of a smile or introduction.

I told her who I was — that I had the donkey that had been taken off of their farm and that I wondered if her husband might be home. I wasn't a reporter, I said. I was a book writer. I was just trying to understand what had happened; I wanted to hear it from him.

She was anxious, I could see that, and was not going to say anything without her husband's approval. He was out back, by the barn, she said. "But he won't talk to you. Couple of reporters called after the police came, and he wouldn't talk to them, either."

I tried to explain that I wasn't here to judge her or her husband, but did not get that chance. "Out back by the barn," she said, closing the door.

That told me that she was afraid, which suggested her husband might be a scary man. I'll confess to having a softer image in my mind. I was trying to set up my theory about mercy by imagining the farmer as a sad and tired soul — cruel not because he was a bad person, but an overwhelmed one.

A man in his tattered overalls, just trying to keep up.

When I rounded the back of the house, he saw me and I saw him at the same time. From his face, I guessed he knew who I was. He was surprised but not shocked; wary but not angry. I'm sure he knew where Simon had been taken, and it would have been easy enough for him to find out what I looked like.

He stood up, backed away from the lawn mower engine he had been oiling, and waited for me to come up to him. I offered my hand, but he held up his, which were covered with oil.

He also appeared to be in his late forties. He wore farmer's clothes, dirty jeans, and a work shirt, but also a pair of incongruously clean pointed leather shoes — definitely not farmer shoes.

He had a full head of jet-black hair, some of which was dangling over his forehead. He kept blowing it out of his eyes. In a different context, I would have tagged him as a lawyer. His hands were dirty and rough like a farmer's, though. He was hard to read.

I introduced myself and said, "Sorry to come here unannounced, but I didn't think you'd talk to me if I called. I'm not here to judge you or cause trouble."

He stood straighter, listened to me, wiped his hands on his jeans. "I'm not going to talk to you," he said. "My lawyer says not to talk to anybody. I'm not going to talk to you."

I took note of the fact that he didn't ask about Simon or seem to want to know anything about him. I volunteered that Simon was doing well, he was okay, it had turned out all right.

I went back to my old reporter's bag of tricks. "Listen, a lot of people had bad things to say about you. I'm a writer and I'm sure I will write about this one day. I don't need to add to the bad things. I'm just curious to know what happened, if you can guide me a bit. Then I'll be out of your way and out of your life."

He looked weary. His eyes seemed cold to me. If he was feeling any emotion he wasn't showing it.

I told him I wasn't going to quote him by name, or reveal his identity or true location. I didn't even need to quote him directly; I just wanted to know his side, to know what had happened.

Most people in conflict with the law feel aggrieved and mistreated, and want to tell their side of things, want their story to get out. He hadn't thrown me out yet, which he could have done right away. I had the sense he wanted to tell me something.

There was a lengthy pause, which I respected. The two of us stood in the back of his farmhouse for the longest time saying nothing. I knew then that he was going to tell me something. Like so many others I had interviewed, he had been waiting for someone to ask him.

He didn't apologize for Simon. He didn't grovel. He said he had never wanted Simon, but to get the horses from the Vermont farmer, he had to take him as well. The farmer pressured him and so he took him. He had a stallion in the corral; he couldn't put Simon, who was also a male, in with him. So he put him in the back pen, a former hog pen, for the moment. It was just supposed to be temporary.

But it stretched out, he said. The farm had been failing for several years; he was about to lose it. He couldn't buy grain on credit, and didn't have enough pasture for his own hay. Last year, he couldn't buy real Christmas presents for his wife and son. The phone rang all day with creditors, and he was trying to make some money buying and selling horses. There was a market overseas.

He barely had enough food for the horses, he said, barely enough for his family. He expected the bank would foreclose on the farm soon; the only thing that kept it alive was that the bank didn't want it any more than he did. He never thought he would be in this position, he said. He never thought he would be so up against it.

I said I would leave, but that I had one last question. "I'm sure you've got a rifle," I said. "Why didn't you just shoot him?"

"I couldn't even look at him," he said. "I fed him as long as I could. I can't talk about this, really. I've said too much." He asked me to leave. I nodded and said good-bye.

The last thing the man said to me was, "I thought he was dead."

I did not get what I was looking for that morning. There were no sobs, no declarations of guilt, no pleas for mercy or understanding. I suppose I had hoped he would break down in tears and I would pat him on the shoulder and nod and say, I understand, I understand.

My ideas about compassion were changing, perhaps even crumbling, by the minute. Compassion was not one thing but many, and it moved around, one second hovering over the farmer, then his son, then Simon.

As I drove back to my farm, I went over the encounter a dozen times. The farmer

161

was defeated, worn down, humiliated and, now, trapped. He couldn't take care of his family. He couldn't keep his farm. He was beyond caring about a hungry donkey. He couldn't feed another animal he didn't want and couldn't sell. He was past caring what people thought, or what I thought.

A part of me wanted to slap the man, to wake him up. Get out of there, I wanted to say. Get your family and get out of there while there is something left of you. Go do something else. Start the work of being a human again.

But this was not for me to do. I remembered his dead eyes. He was beyond reach.

And then I thought about the farmer's wife and son. All this commotion, all this work to save a donkey and bring him back to life.

What about those two? Who was going to worry about them?

Eleven:
The Summons

When I came home from the visit to the farmer, I went out to the barn. I felt a strong need to see Simon. The whole experience had been sad, and I didn't get what I had wanted: a good reason to show mercy and compassion to this man.

Or did I?

I looked up at the hill and saw Lulu and Fanny, up near the gate to the back pasture. They looked uneasy, as if they had spotted something new or strange. Donkeys miss nothing, and if I see them looking hard at something, I know it's something worth paying attention to.

I couldn't see Simon, and this puzzled and worried me. Donkeys are always near one another; they don't go off on their own. I wondered if he was lying down in the pole barn resting. I walked up the soft hill of the pasture, but he wasn't there.

This was alarming. I ran over to where

Lulu and Fanny were standing and looked down the hill. Simon was in the back pasture, by the hay feeder where he was first brought, where he had lain sick for days. I couldn't imagine why he would be there.

I ran down the hill and approached him.

He was sitting upright, in the very spot where I read *Platero and I* to him and brought him his medicines and fed him hay, where I talked to him and, it seemed, he listened to me.

Simon watched me as I ran down the hill. He didn't move as he usually does when he sees me, or bray. He simply sat quietly and looked at me. I was certain something was wrong with him. Donkeys rarely lie down — it makes them vulnerable to predators — and he loved being with Lulu and Fanny.

"Simon, are you okay, boy?" I asked.

I went through the checklist:

His ears were up.

His eyes were wide and clear.

His breathing was steady and strong.

Perhaps he had eaten something that didn't quite agree with him and had just gone back to the spot where he could rest?

I sat down on the ground next to him. I heard a soft bray coming from his snout, almost a wheeze. I thought about calling Ken Norman, or the vet, but he didn't look uncomfortable. I knew what that looked like. I told myself to stop, to not jump into drama, into crisis.

There was something very peaceful about Simon, something expectant, as if he had been waiting for me to come home and find him.

I am wary of such projections, but have also learned that it is as easy to underestimate an animal as it is to overestimate him. I have learned to wait, to listen, to trust my instincts. I didn't feel anything was wrong. It didn't feel right to rush to the phone or send out an SOS. I might be missing something important.

So I decided to do nothing. To wait. We both looked out at the cows grazing in the distant field. Our watchful rooster, Winston the third, was calling the hens to the roost. We watched the chickens making their journey to the safety of the barn. Lulu and Fanny had edged closer through the gate, not wishing to come near but perhaps curious.

How sweet was this soft late afternoon light, a photographer's light. The blackflies were beginning their retreat, the gnats were rising up in clouds — there is always some insect in the warm weather to torment a donkey.

Simon was at ease. He seemed to be soaking up the soft breeze. I went into the barn, opened a can, and grabbed one of his apple cookies. He watched me disappear into the barn — this usually brought him in, as he knows where all the cookies are — but still he remained seated.

I went out and sat down again, and offered him a cookie. He took it gently, and crunched it loudly and slowly while I sat and watched him. He was clearly fine.

So what was happening?

I had a feeling that Simon was waiting for me. He had returned to the spot where he had come for healing, where he had listened to my voice for hours, sat with me night after night.

I remembered once walking into the pasture to see Simon choking on some twigs or brush he had pulled out of the ground. I rushed over to him, put my arms around his neck, reached into the side of his mouth, and pulled out the cluster of roots that were caught in his swollen jaw.

We had been through a lot, me and Simon, and when you are on a journey like that with an animal, you are bound for life. Something in them never forgets it.

I told Simon the story of the visit to the farmer, of our brief conversation. I spoke of the man's coldness, his dead eyes. I told him about the farmer's wife and shared all my impressions of the place.

"So, Simon," I said, "it comes down to this. If you are really compassionate, then you are compassionate to all beings, even those with dead eyes and cold hearts and souls. Something in this man died awhile back, Simon. I don't know if he was born that way, or if life just beat him black and blue, or if struggling on a farm just killed his spirit. I've seen it happen to people. But are you only compassionate to good people, to people you like? It's okay to be compassionate to a raccoon with an infected leg, but not to a human being so lost he would leave you starving to death a few yards away and hope that you were dead?"

I told Simon I didn't really know how to feel, and the truth was, I didn't.

The two of us sat in the pasture and watched the sun set. It felt like forever, but I'm sure it was just an hour or so. Maria came out of the house calling for me; she saw my car and wondered where I was. She sat with us.

As it started to get dark, and we heard the first crickets and frogs down in the meadow, Simon got up on his feet, shook himself off, and walked up the hill to be with Lulu and

Fanny, who waited for him to come through the gate. The three of them walked up toward the top of the pasture, where they often spent the night standing guard over the sheep.

Maria went back into the house, and I stayed behind in the back pasture alone. I was surprised at how emotional a day it had been for me. Simon was clearly well. I looked up, and he was grazing with the other donkeys.

I believe now that Simon had summoned me — had called me to a meditation. Donkeys are the contemplatives of the animal world, and he had called me to him for some purpose that might not be clear to either one of us.

The sound of the crickets and the frogs down by the creek had deepened and become louder, anchoring the night. The gnats and flies were gone. The mosquitoes had risen up, but were held at bay by the breezes that swept the valley for much of the night.

Mercy was very much on my mind. Theologians such as Thomas Aquinas believed that mercy was the greatest of all of the human virtues. It implies a measure of grandeur and nobility. It is the most selfless of human emotions, in that it calls for the generous relief of the needs and miseries of others, out of our own abundance of spirit or wealth. We help others out of our own store of wealth, knowledge, skill, or strength, and if we are truly compassionate, we do so whenever we see sentient beings in need of aid and assistance.

Aquinas did not believe in being merciful to animals out of generosity or compassion for them. He believed we should be merciful to them because it taught us how to be merciful to other human beings.

In his time, most great thinkers believed animals to be inferior to human beings, as they had no conscience and always chose pleasure over virtue. In our time, many people believe animals to be superior to human beings, and sometimes, watching the news, I think they make a good case.

Mercy is a simple thing, really, in Aquinas's time and ours. It is a positive action undertaken for the good of another, to relieve misery. And the worst kind of suffering, Aquinas wrote, is the suffering and misfortune that strikes those who in no way deserve it, the innocent.

This group would include animals, to my mind. Simon was an innocent, a creature of moral value. He had no conception of greed, anger, revenge, or envy. The suffering of animals touches people so deeply, I think, because it is so unprovoked, so impossible to justify.

Animals are dependent on us, they are vulnerable to us; when we mistreat them we are diminishing ourselves, destroying our own humanity.

But it seemed to me, I thought, standing out in my pasture, that the love of animals has made many people less compassionate to humans. The very idea of animal rights in our time is equated with hostility, rage, and self-righteousness.

What was I supposed to feel for the farmer, lost in the story of Simon, and his wife, who was also caught up in it? What is supposed to become of the boy who loved Simon, who tried to feed him, and who set his rescue in motion by making that phone call?

The answer became clear in the pasture. I needed to feel as much compassion for the farmer as I did for Simon, and not because I am morally superior or campaigning for sainthood. I needed to do it for me, for my own soul.

I didn't understand the farmer, and nothing I learned in our talk helped me to understand how he could have gone about his business while this innocent creature lay dying a few feet away. But that was not a reason to hate him, or even to judge him. He deserved as much compassion as Simon did, although no one will come to help him and guide him back to the light. Perhaps he will figure out how to do it himself.

I saw that this contemplation of what measure of compassion is owed to the farmer was a dialogue between Simon and me. It wasn't that he had the words, language, or emotion to join in the discussion or have theories about it. But he had opened up this vein in me. As a person with a lot of anger and judgment inside of him, I found this to be new and challenging terrain.

When I wrote about my reluctance to judge the farmer on my blog, I got a lot of messages from people who were incredulous that I would have any sympathetic feelings for the man after what he had done to Simon. People said that what he had done was too hateful to forgive. But that, I thought, is not compassion.

And why, I kept asking, are people who love animals so angry at people? Animals are perhaps better treated now and more appreciated than at any other time in human history. Why are we so drawn to their abuse and mistreatment, so repelled by our own?

Our society offers us few ways to be

merciful. The poor and the dying are hidden away in ghettos and nursing homes. More and more, we communicate through avatars and devices, and we hear fewer human voices and stories. Our so-called news has become a vehicle for transmitting conflict and tragedy, and we spend more and more time closeted in our homes, flickering screens our most frequent companions.

It's easy to avoid suffering and easier to feel disconnected from the people experiencing it. There are millions of animals in need of care and homes, and it's curious that the idea of animal rescue is so new, even though needy animals have always been around.

Rescuing Simon brought me many gifts. I felt good about doing it; it was immensely satisfying in the most profound way. I was also showered with praise from all over the world.

And you know what? It wasn't very hard to do, it didn't cost much, and it was not complicated if you had a pasture and a barn — I had four. All that was required was hay, several different medicines, and a willingness to put your hands on the tender and private parts of a donkey. I suppose I could admit to a certain squeamishness at the open sores and lice and maggots, but squeamishness is easy to overcome, and I had had a lot of practice dealing with it during my years at the farm.

I did feel generous and noble. Everybody in town knew what we had done for Simon. Everybody thanked me and thought it was a wonderful thing to do. So this is where I put my compassion, my mercy, I thought, here, where it is easy and recognized, not there, out in the country, with that sullen man and his frightened family.

But I was coming to see what mercy and compassion really meant, and where I wanted it to take me.

I went into the house and wrote a letter to the farmer. It said:

Dear _____,
Thanks for talking to me. I appreciate it. I want you to know that Simon is well and I will take good care of him. I suspect you did the best you could. If I can be of any help to you and your family, please feel free to contact me.

And I mailed it off.

The next morning, Simon and I went for a walk in the woods. Except for one standoff — he was determined to veer left to sample some grass he liked the smell of — our walk was easy. He seemed eager and trotted alongside of me. It was warm that morning, and there was a soft breeze blowing down the path. The rustling of the leaves seem to fascinate Simon. I am not sure he had seen them before or paid much attention. For many years, I hadn't, either.

We stopped every now and then so he could lean over and snatch a fat leaf off of a maple tree. He stopped and chewed the leaves thoughtfully. I was beginning to see why so many writers throughout history loved to take walks with donkeys. They are wonderful companions, and they appreciate the natural world, noticing everything in a way that is infectious.

I didn't say much until we turned around and started back toward the farmhouse. By now, the sun was peeking through the forest cover and it seemed as if we were walking into a tunnel of light.

"It's easy to talk about being merciful and compassionate," I said to my donkey. "It's not so easy to figure out how to live that way."

Twelve:
The Different Face
of Compassion

The whole idea of compassion is based
on a keen awareness of the
interdependence of all these living beings,
which are all part of one another and all
involved in one another.
— THOMAS MERTON

There is a particular feeling of self-worth,
even righteousness, that comes from saving
a helpless animal from suffering or mistreatment. When I rescued Simon, there was no
ambivalence or second-guessing; there was
nothing but praise. Praise feels good. I was
learning that compassion also feels good. It
is both healing and affirming, but for me it
was also confusing and troubling. Simon
had me all stirred up.

It's so easy to help an animal in need,
especially if the animal is cute or nice or
amenable to being helped, or shows affection and what we like to call gratitude.

People tell me how grateful Simon seems to me, how appreciative. It's nice to hear, but I've studied and lived with animals long enough to know I have no idea what Simon is really thinking.

Gratitude is a very human kind of emotion. It requires a sense of narrative and reasoning I don't believe animals have. When animals are fed and given attention — fresh hay and an apple a day will do it — they attach very powerfully to the people nurturing them. Their lives depend on it; their instincts proffer it. Dogs and donkeys have been around people a very long time — they know the game. Simon plays me like a Stradivarius, braying and sighing whenever he sees me until he gets a cookie or a carrot. If someone else comes along with a cookie or a carrot, he is off like a shot.

Perhaps the longing look Simon gives me is gratitude; perhaps it's just the excitement any domesticated animal has learned to display when food or attention is in the picture. This may sound cynical, but it is not really. Simon is attached to me; he is also attached to the many hundreds of other people who visit and bring him carrots and treats. We see what we want to see and need to see. This is the role animals play in our distracted and intense world.

Animals can't leave, talk back, disagree, or challenge our assistance. There are few, if any, laws or regulations governing caring for them. They can't sue us if something gets screwed up or go on Facebook and air their grievances.

As I thought about it, I realized that I was pretty careful in my choice of compassionate opportunities. I didn't feel too much compassion for snakes or coyotes, cows or rabid raccoons and skunks. I wondered how much compassion I would have felt for Simon had he been ill-tempered or resistant to treatment, if he hadn't watched me carefully with his big brown eyes as I read to him, or loved children and visitors so much.

When it came to my being compassionate toward people, I was even more selective, as Simon helped me to see. There was a sweet woman down the road with cancer, and I took her food and offered to help her every day. Another neighbor was a mean drunk living alone in poverty. I never thought of taking him food or visiting his house.

I began to see I was making decisions about compassion, and recalibrating those decisions all the time. For instance, we had a big beautiful rooster named Strut, who I took a lot of photos of and put them up on my blog. Eventually he began to turn aggressive, as many roosters do, and attacked Maria one afternoon. The attack was disturbing. Strut threw himself suddenly at Maria's legs as she walked by, raking her with his beak and claws, attacking again and again, even after she kicked at him and blocked him with a bucket.

Before she got away from him, her legs were covered with blood and scratches. Maria is the kind of person who rehomes spiders and moths; compassion comes much more naturally to her than to me. Still, she was shaken by the attack.

I went into the house, got my .22 rifle, loaded it, and walked out in the pasture where Strut was pecking for bugs with his hens. I shot him through the heart, killing him almost instantly.

When I wrote about this on my blog, I got many messages of understanding from farmers who had known roosters and had been through the same experience, and many from people with pets who expressed outrage that I would kill the rooster rather than rehome him or confine or separate him in some way.

"I suppose," one woman fumed, "you would shoot a sheep if she attacked your wife." Well, yes, I thought, I would.

None of those people expressed any concern or compassion for Maria or for the idea that the safety of a human is of equal importance to the well-being of a rooster.

So there were different dimensions to my practice of compassion: While I tended to be compassionate to people and animals I liked and who liked me, I found it hard to be compassionate or empathetic to people whose beliefs and actions were offensive or disturbing to me.

Compassion, like freedom of speech, is one of those ideas we all love to talk about until something vile happens, then not so much.

And yet, I thought, wasn't compassion really about empathizing on a broader scale than that? Simon had entered my interior world. Empathizing with him was easy; he touched on many of my own painful childhood issues — loneliness, abandonment, neglect, abuse. I didn't experience the same things he had, but I did experience what I imagined were some of the things he suffered. I related to them.

Strut didn't receive the same empathy, and I can't say I regret it, either.

I began reading the works of some strong thinkers on compassion — the Dalai Lama, Thomas Merton, Saint Francis of Assisi, Plato, Albert Einstein, Albert Schweitzer —

and I kept running across another view of it. Compassion is not really about our personal interior world but the exterior one. It extends to living things beyond our yards and pastures. It extends to people as well as animals, encompassing things we don't like as well as things we do: animals that are not cute and endearing, but are simply suffering and in need.

My ideas about compassion were small and immediate — my interior world — but compassion was a much bigger and more complex idea than that. I did not come close to understanding it yet — not in me, not in the world beyond.

When I looked at the news, I saw little compassion mirrored back at me. In fact, whenever I looked at news from Washington, I saw none. Our world is not very compassionate. I wonder sometimes if anyone apart from the Dalai Lama can be deeply and consistently compassionate. And even he often says, in his speeches and memoirs, that he is not nearly as patient or compassionate as he would like to be.

Is compassion some ephemeral and unachievable goal for people, or is it really possible?

Many of our leaders do not seem able to put themselves in another's shoes; instead they relentlessly attack and demonize the people standing in front of them. Religion often seems riddled with conflict and judgment to me — at least until Pope Francis appeared and seemed to touch a deep global need for compassion and empathy.

If the people leading the world didn't feel much compassion, what hope was there for me? Okay, I saved a donkey, but that will not necessarily alter the nature of the world. Or will it?

Standing in the pasture, waiting for Simon to bray to me and come down to get his morning apple, maybe get some balm rubbed on his wounds, I think I understood that compassion was a powerful and important goal, like spirituality: perhaps a path that never ended, a journey that was never over.

Humans have a need for compassion, but they also have a lot of anger, envy, frustration, and resentment, all the enemies of compassion.

I liked Merton's call to awareness. For me the process had begun. I was aware of compassion, of its ubiquity and interdependence. A donkey in trouble had begun the process for me, and I had absolutely no idea how far I would go with it, or even should.

Merton's idea — the interdependence of

all things — was something I found in Saint Francis, Einstein, and in almost all of the great writings about compassion. "In the first step toward a compassionate heart," wrote the Dalai Lama, "we must develop our empathy or closeness to others. . . . The closer we are to a person, the more unbearable we find that person's suffering." It is not, says the Dalai Lama, a question of physical proximity; it is a feeling of responsibility.

We are not alone. We are all connected. Me, Simon, the farmer, the state police, all of the donkeys and people of the world, we are one thing. I love this idea. It is powerful and stirring, yet it is not what I feel inside of my head, not what I see in the outside world, not what is on the news, in all those arguments and press conferences out of Washington, in all those pious and often angry declarations I hear from people who call themselves religious.

I wonder how Saint Thomas Aquinas might have dealt with one of the dominant ideas of our time, the Facebook idea, the notion of interconnectedness, of one family, of interdependence taken to an almost unimaginable level — a billion people connected to each other. Is a connected medium the same as a compassionate one? I don't think so.

Soon after Simon came to the farm, I was invited to do a Q & A with an animal rescue site on Facebook. The page had two hundred thousand likes and it was teeming with photos, videos, and commentary about animal rescue, and almost all of it was enraged, furious. It seemed to me to be a hive of angry bees.

Although a number of people thanked me for saving Simon, most of the comments on the page offered horror stories of animals abused, mistreated, neglected, or abandoned, and there was nothing but rage and contempt for the human beings of the world presumably responsible for all of this cruelty.

I asked myself a question: Can you love an animal and hate people and be compassionate?

If we are all one, part of the same interconnected system, why do we feel so much for the animal who is mistreated but so little for the human beings who mistreat them?

Looking at Simon, I could not help but wonder about his farmer. I was shocked at the concern I felt for him. I had intuitively done just what the Dalai Lama was suggesting. I recognized the gravity of his misery, the suffering that must have occurred for him to lose his humanity in this way.

Perhaps I was able to do this because I had a farm. I am a writer, not a farmer, but I have many friends who are farmers, and I have seen up close the grinding brutality of their lives, the constant struggle, the filth, disease, mechanical and money issues, the wrestling with bureaucracies and regulations, all the things that make their lives such a challenge.

For several years, I have photographed farmers in their struggles, and so I possessed the physical and emotional closeness the Dalai Lama is talking about when it comes to compassion.

I could almost feel Simon's farmer's struggle to survive, day after day, year after year, to the point that his exhaustion and frustration might have simply drained his soul of energy and reason.

I shared these thoughts on the rescue website, and the response was fast, furious, and merciless. The farmer was an animal, a monster; he should be jailed, punished, tortured, even killed. No one offered a single line of compassion or understanding or concern for him, or for his son, who had bravely helped Simon when he was starving.

The hatred and fury were shocking to me,

disturbing; this idea of rescue was not compassionate for me. I withdrew from it; it wasn't where Simon's experience was taking me. Something inside of me has always rebelled at the idea that loving animals justifies hating people.

With Simon, I had taken a big step toward a compassionate heart. I saw, in my mind, felt in my heart, this idea of interdependence, this sense of my experience with Simon being connected to the wider world.

As we treat one creature, we treat all creatures. As we free ourselves of judgment, we learn what compassion is and how to feel it.

Our task, wrote Einstein, is to liberate ourselves by widening our circle of compassion to embrace all living creatures and the whole of nature and its beauty.

I loved this idea. This was where I wanted to go, where Simon was meant to lead me. Perhaps this is why he had come, and why I had accepted him so eagerly into my life and embraced his healing so passionately. Perhaps this is why he opened me up.

But it was also humbling for me. My spirit was not remotely ready to stretch to so vast and all-encompassing an embrace. It would require as much change as anything I had ever attempted in my life.

I am not the Dalai Lama, not Merton, and surely no Einstein. The voice in my head was small and soft: "What's the big deal? He's just a donkey."

It is fashionable to quote brilliant people and ignore what they say. Reading Merton's call to compassion, I wondered if Simon and I were too small to quite grasp it, let alone live it.

Pressed by the details of ordinary life — work, money, family, friends, health — my consciousness is rarely large enough to encounter the entire universe of beings. I am touched by the call to recognize that we are all one, but I am hard-pressed to keep such a huge concept in the forefront of my brain as I go about my life, which is filled with small things. And I was discouraged by the hard reality of what I saw in the exterior world, the one beyond Simon and me.

■ ■ ■ ■

PART III
THE MEANING
OF COMPASSION

■ ■ ■ ■

THIRTEEN: ROCKY

If Simon began teaching me the meaning of compassion, Rocky, a small blind pony, was to be one of my biggest and most challenging lessons.

In the winter of 2010, the blizzards came week after week, dumping so much snow in parts of the Northeast that the plows had no place to put it. All of the farmers I knew were worried about their barns, and for good reason.

Most barns are old, built by friends and neighbors long ago, with thin rafters and slate or shingle roofs. Many of these barns were made from cedar planks, because the farmers had a tool called an adze that split cedar trees easily. Typically, barn roofs are slanted so that the snow will slide off onto the ground, but this winter, the heavy snow was wet and, thanks to climate change, the temperatures varied wildly. It snowed, then warmed up a bit, then froze. Then more snow came and piled on. You could see it driving by: huge amounts of snow piled up on barn roofs, no easy or safe way to get it off.

It was the worst possible combination for the barn roofs in my area. You could almost hear the barns and rooftops groaning under all of the weight.

It was a rough winter on my farm, and we checked the barns almost every day. Our slate roofs held, although when the snow did slide off, it was so heavy it was dangerous to be near when it fell, and many of the slate tiles came with it.

Several times a week, I drove down Route 22 in Washington County to go shopping, visit friends, get to the hardware store.

I love old barns and have taken thousands of photos of them. When I walk into a barn, the farmers usually nod and wave to me, and when I ask permission to take a photo, they all say, "Sure, help yourself." No farmer has ever asked me what I am doing with the photos or even why I am taking them.

So it was wrenching when the barns started falling. By February and early March, it was impossible to go more than a few miles without seeing a big old beautiful barn toppled over.

And these, we all knew, were not temporary losses. Nobody built big cedar barns any longer. The wood was too expensive, insurance was too high, and many of them were on properties that were no longer farms but second homes or country residences. When farmers needed new barns, they used aluminum or other metal structures or even plastic tarpaulins.

I drove by a beautiful old farmhouse on Route 22 and saw that one of its two barns had collapsed. Most of these old barns were filled with junk. If the farmers were lucky, scrappers came by to take the metal inside in exchange for hauling off the wood. Some carpenters love using old barn wood for their restoration projects and will sometimes pay for a collapsed barn's demolition.

But most of the barns just began rotting where they fell, and most of them are there still, ghosts from another world.

I must have driven by that old white farmhouse a hundred times without ever really looking at it. In the spring of 2011, after Simon had been with us for a few months, I was driving northbound on Route 22 and I looked over at the fallen barn — it framed the old farmhouse in an evocative way, making a statement about what I perceived to be the abandonment of rural life by the country's political and economic system.

It was surprising to me, but when I looked this time, I was startled to see Simon standing in front of the barn, head down, grazing on the new grass coming up.

I couldn't imagine what he might be doing there, how he got there, or how a donkey that looked so much like him could be in that pasture and I never saw or noticed him before.

I wondered if I was tired or woozy. I pulled over to the side of the road and then pulled into the driveway in front of the old farmhouse. It was curious. There were no cars, no signs of life. When I got out of my car, I saw that the donkey was not a donkey, but a pony, an old Appaloosa pony. I remember that moment so clearly. It was compassion I felt looking out at that scene, the same compassion I felt for Simon. This feeling was to alter my life.

There was something both poignant and powerful about the image; the horse must have been there all winter, and for many winters before that, and yet I had never noticed him. Why did I see him now? And why would I see Simon standing there, when the pony looked nothing like Simon? The pony's long coat was a yellowish white.

I could see even from that distance — about one hundred yards — that he was covered in burrs, and his fur was matted. Perhaps this was his barn that had fallen? I wondered if he had any other shelter. A second barn was standing to the left of the pony, weathered but intact.

Simon had sensitized me to the plight of animals on farms. No one had noticed him, either, lying nearly dead in his pen, and if someone hadn't finally called the police, he would not be alive.

Looking more closely, I saw that the pony was very old, and that he appeared well fed. I called out to him, "Hey, pony," and he looked back and forth, as if he could not quite locate me.

I went to the front door and knocked. I saw lights on inside and thought I heard a radio playing. I knocked a few times and waited about five minutes. I wanted to take a photo of that old pony standing in front of his collapsed barn. It was a metaphor for rural life, I thought. It was an emotional image, and timeless, and it touched my heart. But I wanted to ask permission. Even when it appeared that nobody was home, I never went on anybody's property without asking permission. I had never been denied it, but I still wanted to ask.

As I turned to leave, disappointed, the door opened, and an older woman stepped out. She was quite beautiful — erect, tall, with white hair. She looked at me curiously, but her eyes were blue and piercing. I guessed her to be in her late sixties. She was 102, as she later told me. Her name was Florence Walrath.

She loved horses — had had them all of her life, she said. She was one of the founders of the Cambridge Saddle Club. The pony's name was Rocky. "He doesn't look as good now as he once did," she said. "But then, neither do I," she added, smiling.

Florence had a remarkable presence. Something about her commanded attention; she had an uncommon dignity and confidence.

I saw right away that she had trouble hearing me, but I pointed to the camera and then at Rocky, and she nodded and said she understood.

"Well," she said. "I'm deaf and Rocky is blind. He's thirty-three years old, and he knows his way around the pasture. You are welcome to take his picture. I won't let you take mine," she said, and she shook my hand and began to close the door. "Me and Rocky, we're just riding it out together."

I went over to the pasture gate and took a few shots. It was easy to compose that photo, I remember. Rocky was grazing with his head down right in front of the collapsed barn, which I could see had once been quite beautiful.

A maple tree stood in front of the gate, creating a perfect composition. The surviving barn was on the left, its red wall framing the left sight of the shot.

There was this old pony in front of a collapsed barn, both symbols in their own way of a lost world. The photo affected me. It said much about the country, about rural life and its plight. Why had I not seen this before, or felt it before?

I suppose that Simon was the reason. I guessed it then; I know it now. Animals have always been powerful symbols for people: magical helpers, protectors, guides, and companions. A friend of mine, a shaman, e-mailed me that year to tell me that Simon had appeared as a spirit guide for me, to lead me to new experience, to open me up to feeling and emotion. Maybe so.

I went to visit Rocky regularly after that first visit. Florence Walrath often came out onto the porch to talk to me. She was getting frail, weaker, and she could not hear or see well. Still, I valued the brief contact we had. She was a charismatic, strong person. She told me she would never leave her home, despite her failing health. I believed her.

Rocky had about five or six acres to roam in, and was kept outside without shelter. Florence said she couldn't bear to part with him, and was losing the energy to take care of him. I would come by with some apples, walk to the fence, and call out his name. In the beginning he would turn and hide behind the barn when he heard me.

Eventually he came close and I climbed the fence — most of it had fallen apart, leaving the pasture open to the road. After a few weeks, Rocky came over to me, sniffing, and I handed him the sliced apple open in my palm. He searched for it with his nose, took it gently, then put it on the ground where he could break it up and chew it.

He had lived alone in that pasture for half his life, always without shelter. He found his own water, grazed in his own spots around the pasture. In the winter, he was given grain and thrown hay out of the back of the barn. The men at the feed store still talk about going out to Florence's farm with huge bags of grain for Rocky, and if the weather was bad, finding hundred-year-old Florence shoveling a path for them in the snow. Some woman, they said.

Florence loved Rocky, but in the particular way of the practical country farm girl. Compassion, for her, was not gourmet treats, blankets and heaters, visits from the vet, or worries about how he was faring in the rain or snow. Florence's gift to Rocky was life. Beyond that he was pretty much on his own.

When I first put photos of Rocky up on my website and on my Facebook page, I was inundated with messages of concern for him. Poor pony, a blind creature out on his own, his barn collapsed. Could I save him? Bring him to a rescue facility? Take him to my farm? Build him a new barn? Get him to shelter?

Rocky never seemed needy to me, quite the opposite. He was astonishingly skilled at getting around and taking care of himself. He seemed to have made a series of paths around the property and he followed them. One was out to the south pasture, out near the fence (which had no wire in it — Rocky could have walked out any time but knew not to). Another led to the rear of the farm where there was water running in a stream.

Yet for so many people, compassion meant seeing him as helpless and in need of rescue. From the first, I was bombarded with messages about helping Rocky, getting him a new barn, good grain, even a new home.

For Florence, who loved Rocky dearly, compassion was much simpler. He had his own pasture, a stream, some hay in the winter, the basic elements of life. He was free to live his life as a pony. Florence had no regrets or guilt about that.

In bad weather, Rocky hugged the rear of the barn, avoiding the worst of the wind and snow. He led a life of complete freedom, going where he wanted when he wanted, and the ground was safe and familiar to him. Even if Florence could no longer take meticulous care of him, she had loved horses all of her life, and the two of them seemed powerfully aware of each other.

To me, and to many of the farmers I knew in the area, Rocky had a great life. He lived as freely and safely as any animal did in the wild, and the farmers always talked about how lucky he was.

I did have my own concerns about Rocky, however. I saw that his teeth were bad and needed work. His hooves had not been trimmed in years. There were saw burrs and thistles all over his coat, and cuts and scrapes from walking blind into tree limbs and brush. I wondered if his vision could be helped, or if he was totally blind. Nobody really knew.

I came to see Rocky almost every day, and then Maria came to join me. She fell immediately and hopelessly in love with Rocky. Neither of us had ever had a horse. Although horses were equines like donkeys, they were very different.

Maria loved the donkeys, and they loved her back. She has a particular gift for communicating with animals — a way of listening to them and approaching them gently and calmly. When she walks out of the farmhouse, every animal on the farm starts meowing, braying, or barking.

When we came up to Rocky's fence we always held out apples and carrots. Rocky would approach, use his nose and ears to locate us, and then come close. Eventually, we would climb over the fence and come up to him, calling his name so he could hear us and figure out where we were.

Food is a language with animals; I have never known one that did not bond to people who fed them regularly. We brought Rocky grain to fatten him up. Our connection to Rocky grew stronger, and there were many sweet afternoons out behind the barns. Rocky loved to walk with us behind the farmhouse in the fields. When it snowed or rained, we made sure to stop by and check on him. There were old horse and cow stalls in the barn, but they were filled with junk and old furniture, and we knew Florence could not have handled the manure and the other problems that putting Rocky in the stall would cause.

Just as Simon brayed, Rocky neighed when we pulled into the driveway. He knew the sound of our cars and the sound of our voices. He loved Maria, and would almost sigh in contentment when she brushed him, sang to him, and talked to him. It was a free life, we thought, but perhaps a lonely life. Horses, like donkeys, are herd animals and love company. Wouldn't it be nice, Maria and I often said to each other, if the donkeys or sheep were here to keep Rocky company? He could follow them around and perhaps find new grazing areas.

Maria felt a profound compassion for Rocky; she connected to him in a way I had not seen her ever connect to an animal besides her dog Frieda. His blindness, his age, and his gentleness all touched her deeply.

Maria and I are very different in our approaches to animals. Animals such as dogs and horses and donkeys do share one thing — they are intuitive readers of human emotion. I think men in general, me in particular, are less open emotionally than many women. One of the ways in which animals communicate is through emotion — they smell, see, and sense our moods.

Maria is an intensely and overtly emotional person. She will often cry — it is not a sad thing, just a way of expressing herself. She cries in the same way some people talk. She has powerful nurturing and intuitive instincts, and unlike me, hers are right out in the open. She is an artist, and she uses these feelings to create her work and express herself.

She has a powerful way with animals; she is both a healer and a whisperer. She seems to understand how to approach them in an open, nonthreatening, and yet affectionate way. She speaks to animals in a soft but enthusiastic voice that always seems to attract and calm them. She understands the power of food in human–animal connections, and she understands as well how to be still around animals, to let them smell her, approach her, relax around her. They are at ease with her. They tolerate her touching them, brushing them. There is no wariness.

It seemed that Rocky had not been touched for a long time, perhaps in years. It took a month or so before he began to visibly attach to Maria. He became comfortable with her. While he always let me approach him or take his photo, he got skittish if I tried to touch him or brush him.

That was not the case with Maria. She began talking to Rocky the second she entered the pasture. Maria seemed to instinctively know how to reach an animal like Rocky. As she got close, she kept speaking to him, so he could locate her and know where she was. She is exquisitely sensitive to others and knew a blind animal would be comforted by hearing a constant voice.

"Hey, Rocky," Maria would say in her soft voice. "How's my little pony?"

As Rocky became more comfortable with us, and we with him, I saw that Maria was also becoming much more deeply attached to him. At first, she approached him tentatively, holding an apple out with her hand. She was soft-spoken and, like me, reluctant to show too much enthusiasm or reveal too much of herself.

A friend of ours, Paula Josa-Jones, a longtime horse lover, came up to visit us, and we took her to see Rocky. Maria and I were both amazed at how emotive she was, at how much feeling she showed him, how enthusiastically she was moving her body and her hands. She was much more verbal than Maria and I had been, her voice pitched higher and louder than ours.

She touched him along the neck, brushed him, and rubbed her hands along his back.

Rocky seemed to revel in this burst of energy and demonstrative show of affection. Maria and I felt sluggish in comparison, almost like mutes. And it was striking to see how Rocky responded. He snuggled up to Paula, almost danced in response to her. He became more animated; her attention seemed to bring him back to an older, more comfortable and happy place.

Maria changed after that. She also became more emotive, allowing herself to talk to Rocky in a different voice: to show, not just speak, her affection for him, to move with him and around him. And Rocky changed as well. If he was comfortable around Maria before, he seemed to adore her now. He whinnied loudly when he heard her voice, came running to see her, pressed his head against her, and stood still for long minutes while she talked to him, sang to him, and brushed the burrs out of his mane and coat.

He was shaggy and unkempt when we first met him, but under Maria's careful ministrations, he looked sleek and clean again, and seemed to feel better. He was livelier, clearly affectionate. It was an amazing thing to see, the way these two loving creatures took to each other. I think Rocky did for Maria what Simon had done for me: he opened her up and challenged her to be more outgoing, less guarded with her emotions.

We went on walks with Rocky down to his creek on his path. He seemed an eager tour guide, happy to show us his world, a place he had occupied for more than thirty years, half of them alone.

Rocky's world was a beautiful place, and his ability to deal with his blindness was a powerful thing to see. Sometimes we would see him bang into the side of the barn, or a fence post, but generally he knew every foot of the pasture, where to walk, when to stop. Rocky was a healthy, happy pony.

But I was not able to convince many animal lovers on the Internet. Every day I was besieged with messages and e-mails begging me to find him shelter, to get him to another farm, to build a special barn and enclosure for him. I tried to explain that this was a loved animal, a lucky animal; that he led as good a life as any pony in the world. But the schism in understanding was too wide, and I gave up the argument.

In the animal rescue world, compassion often means emotionalizing. It means keeping animals alive by any means at all costs, whereas in what I call the real world of real animals, it was much more complex than that, at least to me.

Florence told me that she had once thought about putting Rocky down. She thought it might be the most compassionate thing to do to an animal living outdoors by himself, with an older person who couldn't do much more than feed him and visit him. She said she couldn't bring herself to do it.

But Florence never really saw Rocky as piteous, and neither did I. More and more, we seem to need to see pets and animals as piteous and troubled, perhaps so that we have a reason to be loving and nurturing, opportunities for which are increasingly dwindling in our culture. I never felt Rocky was in dire trouble on that farm. He might have been made more comfortable, but Florence didn't have the money to do that. Rocky loved Florence, and she loved him. True, he did not have some of the amenities pets have — a warm cozy room, lots of attention, regular checkups by a vet. But he had more than enough. How could I explain that it would have been cruel to move an aging, blind pony to another farm? To change his routines? It was inspiring to see the way he navigated those paths, finding the water stream even in winter.

Maria and I were both in love with him, as we were with Simon. Although these two animals were different, they touched deep chords in us, chords of mercy and compassion.

FOURTEEN:
THE TAO OF RED

In the same way that I never would have noticed Rocky if it weren't for Simon, I doubt that I would ever have agreed to take Red if it hadn't been for Simon. I find that men do not open up easily, and I surely spent too much of my life in a tight and closed knot. Opening up is risky. It means accepting new experiences, considering other possibilities. Simon helped me to do that.

I tend to divide my life into two parts — closed and open — and I am still shocked at how the process of opening up released a floodgate of good and meaningful things, things I have always wanted in my life but could not find.

As I approached sixty, my life came apart. An accumulation of ignored or neglected problems finally worked together to break me down — perhaps the most effective means of opening up that there is.

When you are living in panic, your life going to pieces, then suddenly there is the necessary motivation to open up and get to work. Simon made my true path clear, quite unintentionally. He began an era in which I started doing things I formerly thought impossible. Like taking in a donkey that was at death's door. Like deciding at age sixty-one that I wanted love in my life again. Like befriending a blind pony. Like meditating again. Like getting a dog from a woman who said, "God wants you to have him." It's a long and important list.

So my experience with Simon was, for me, about deepening the miraculous process of opening myself up to the possibilities of life, of taking emotional risks and chances. The dangers are considerable, I learned, the rewards unimaginable, especially in our fearful and fragmented world.

In recent years, I've come to believe in the idea of spirit animals. They enter your life when you are ready; they leave when it is time. Such was the case with my two border collies, Rose and Izzy.

I woke up one night in the winter of 2011 with a powerful and frightening feeling that something was wrong with Rose — that she was in trouble. I dressed hurriedly and went downstairs. I went room to room and could not find her, and, more alarming, she didn't answer my call for her. Rose was always by my side in a flash when I said her name; she was always eager to get out and work, like most border collies. I searched the living room, my office, the family room at the back of the house, and then, as an afterthought, went out to the mudroom behind the kitchen, right by the back door. This is often where I found Rose waiting to be let out to go to the pasture.

I knew the minute I saw her lying on the floor that she was dying. This animal had been by my side through so much, from my first day at the farm. She was so filled with energy and intelligence and determination and pride. When I saw her lying on her side in a pool of vomit, glassy-eyed and trembling, I just knew she was letting go of life.

I will never forget that moment. I heard Rose speaking so clearly to me, saying in a matter-of-fact voice, "Help me, help me." I knew she wanted to leave the world in dignity — that her work was done and she was pleading with me to help her go.

We got to the vet that morning, and she agreed that Rose was very sick. Neither of us wanted to subject her to the invasive and painful tests that would tell us more. That's the thing about animals, really. They are never static, at least not for long. Their comings and goings are never really explicable to us, as smart as we think we are. Simon should have been dead, but he was not. Border collies live forever, and Rose was healthy, happy, and active. The vet was stymied. Rose just seemed to wither. It might be something neurological, she said. It was hard to say without a lot of tests. I didn't want to do that to Rose, and I felt her telling me very clearly that she was done. She was tired. She was ready to go, and I decided to honor that. I chose not to be selfish. I wanted her to leave the world in dignity, she was so proud and dignified and brave a dog. A few days later, she was gone, euthanized on the floor at our vet's office, having led a full and glorious life.

Izzy was different. I don't think he wanted to go; I don't think he was ready. I saw him struggling to walk on the path one day, and felt the lumps growing around his throat. I knew it had to be cancer, and it was: advanced lymphoma. The vet did a biopsy and said he had a few weeks to live at most, and, if we allowed it, he would live those weeks in pain. So six months after Rose died, we put Izzy down.

Izzy was a different dog than Rose. He was a lover, not a worker; a people dog, not a sheep dog. He and I became hospice volunteers together just after my divorce, when my life seemed so bleak and empty. Izzy and our work together brought me back from the edge. We helped people on the true edge of life leave the world peacefully and in comfort.

It was a shock to me to lose two such wonderful dogs within a few months of each other. I expected them both to live for many years. I had this recurring feeling that as my life changed — I was no longer alone on the farm; Maria had entered my life — and as I became saner and more grounded, that Rose's mission had to change. My idea, maybe it was a fantasy, was that she had decided to go live and work with someone else, someone needier.

In the days and weeks after Rose died, this idea became more focused in my mind. I believed it to be true. I think Izzy just got sick and died. I never felt he was ready to leave. He loved his hospice work, chasing sunsets with me as I photographed them, and his time with Maria on the farm. Izzy was a creature of great joy, and sometimes life simply happens. I think of Rose and Izzy often, not in grief but in gratitude. I am grateful to have had two such dogs, grateful that they both got to live their lives as dogs as fully and freely as it is possible to do in our world.

And again, there was Simon's spirit in my head. I can't speak for what's inside of his genial consciousness, but I can speak to what was inside of mine. From the first, I was struck by what I saw as the great trait of acceptance in Simon. People always spoke of him as being abused, rescued, or neglected, but I saw no sign that Simon thought of himself in that way. Simon immediately got down to the basics of life — eating, walking, pursuing the girls, getting his ration of carrots and apples, getting brushed and fussed over.

He got on with life. He did not waste his precious time being angry at the farmer or complaining about his fate. His call to life was very real. He seemed to me set on enjoying every second of his time here.

Unquestionably, this affected my view of the loss of Rose and Izzy. I do not adhere to the idea that "it's just a dog" when a beloved pet dies. Rose and Izzy were as important to me and my life as most of the human beings I have known. They affected my life. They changed it.

But Simon helped me understand that the

joy of life is more important than the loss of it. I honored Rose and Izzy, mourned them and cried for them, but like Simon, I was not going to spend my life lamenting what I did not have. I wanted to appreciate and enjoy the many riches I did have.

Grief is a personal, highly individual thing. Everyone experiences it in their own way; everyone heals in their own way.

After these two wonderful dogs died, I started thinking about another one, as I tend to do when I lose a dog. Many people tell me they are so heartbroken over the death of a dog that they can't bear to get another one. That always makes me sad, especially when so many millions of dogs languish in shelters awaiting homes, often for years.

I began a casual search. A border collie kept coming to mind. I always seem drawn to border collies. They seem to think and function like I do. They're a bit distracted, their multi-track minds always racing; they could probably be diagnosed with attention deficit disorder. I like their enthusiasm for life, their work ethic, their intelligence, and their craziness. All border collies and their owners are a little bit crazy, I find. It works for both species.

I trawled through breeders' websites and

left some phone and e-mail messages. Just sniffing around. My favorite way to get a dog is through a good and experienced breeder. Although border collies are often in need of rescue, for a working farm dog, I need to be certain of temperament and genetics. I was in no rush. We had plenty of animals to take care of and we had two wonderful dogs, Lenore and Frieda, both of whom were enjoying all the attention they were getting.

In the spring of 2012, I got an e-mail from Dr. Karen Thompson, a much loved and respected border collie breeder in Virginia. She got right to the point. She had a seven-year-old red-coated border collie from County Tyrone, Ireland, she said. He had had a rough time — had been brought to the United States and had come to her. Those were all of the details I was to get at that time. He was a fine working dog, she said, eager to please, generous of nature, professional, and well trained. His outruns were a bit on the wide side. She loved the dog and had not been able to part with him. She had driven him to a home in the South and then, unable to sleep for days, she drove back and brought him home. He was much loved, she said, and no one who knew him wanted him to leave.

But, she said, she knew of my hospice work with my border collie Izzy since she had read my book *Izzy & Lenore*. She believed Red was a natural for that work. She knew I had some sheep, and that would be great, but she wanted more than that for Red.

She wanted him to have a rounded life, a balanced life, one beyond the pasture. She worked him regularly with her sheep, but there were a lot of dogs coming and going on her farm, and she couldn't give him the life I might be able to give him.

"God wants you to have Red," she said. "He wants him to be your dog." I was surprised by this and taken aback. I wondered if Karen was a little strange. God had never been involved in my choice of dogs, at least as far as I knew. The idea made me nervous.

Karen sent me a video of Red working the sheep. A rocket dog, I thought, watching him shoot out on a spectacular outrun around some sheep. He knew his stuff, and he seemed to be an eager, responsive dog. I was impressed and intrigued. I thought about it for a long time, and eventually told Karen that I would take Red.

I have had dogs for much of my life, but my true life with them began when I bought a cabin in upstate New York to write a book there and I brought two yellow labs, Julius and Stanley, with me for company. They were as much a part of the process — more, really — than my computer. Together, we had all kinds of experiences on that mountaintop, but when I returned to New Jersey, where my family was, our lives together shrank — walks, the backyard, time in the house.

Julius and Stanley had walked with me on the mountaintop; my day had begun with them. They sat by my feet while I worked. They eased the loneliness of a long, hard winter, making it bearable, even meaningful. They were never, for me, a substitute for human beings, but still, they were a living and loving force that anchored my creativity and grounded me. I opened myself up to them, and they to me. This is what happened, too, on a different, more spiritual level, with Simon. The dogs opened the door; Simon walked through it.

And now here was Red, a creature from Ireland, a quirky and soulful little border collie who just fused with me as if we had always been together. A working dog and farm dog, Red had never lived inside of a home before and struggled at first with some of the details of domestic American dog life. He didn't quite get glass and ran into the window frames around our doors. When he tried to jump on the bed, he would misjudge the distances and go sailing over the bed and onto the floor. He was terrified of linoleum and didn't recognize it as ground. He would freeze when he came to it, then rush across.

He sometimes heard commands and strange sounds in his sleep, and if I was running a video of any kind, he'd go into his border collie crouch and start doing outruns around the living room floor. The wind obsessed and disturbed him, and he would stare up in the skies looking to see where it came from. I often said to Maria that Red was not like the other children. Perhaps this is why I loved him so much and identified with him from the start.

Red is often so eager to jump into the backseat of the car that he misses and plows into the open door, bouncing off it, shaking himself off, and trying again. If he wants to see me, and Lenore or Frieda is lying in front of me, he simply jumps on the other dog and sits there or walks right over her. This doesn't sit well with Frieda. She roars at Red, but he doesn't seem to notice.

Red is an amazing working dog, instantly responsive, smart and reliable. And he has a heart and soul as big and generous as any dog I have known. Red will often appear to be peacemaking, helping another animal out. Perhaps he views this as just another form of work. Perhaps he is reading my mind, as he has an intuitive habit of doing. Red is not like Simon. He is obedient, attentive, and eager to please. Simon is eager to please when he is in the mood, not so eager when he isn't. It's odd, but true, that I love Red because he wants to please me, and I love Simon because he often doesn't care to please me.

Red was confused and distracted when he came to me, and I often thought of his long journey from Ireland to Virginia to me. I was told he had been brutally beaten, and I could see he was often anxious and very wary of sticks.

Could I deepen this idea of partnership with this dog? Could I replicate the sense of exploration Jiménez had with Platero, and that I had with Simon?

The morning after Red arrived, I took him out to the pasture. As we approached the gate, he went into a herding crouch, froze, and stared at the sheep. I opened the gate and realized I didn't know the herding commands he had been taught. I called Dr. Thompson on my cell phone and she told me to stand to the right of Red and say "Come bye." I did, and he took off like a guided missile. He made a sweeping and spectacular outrun wide of the sheep and drove them right to me.

When he made his way back to me, he was transformed. He was looking straight into my eyes. His world had returned to its proper order. He was adoring me in that particular way border collies have of worshipping whoever takes them to sheep.

Until he came to my farm, Red had either been out working sheep or in a crate. He was not housebroken. Dr. Thompson's hope was that Red's life could be broadened, and it was my wish, too. Of course, I ended up being broadened as much as he was, possibly more.

From that first day, Red went everywhere with me. He walked into a farm stand nearby, found the girls behind the cash register and, while I stuffed my corn and vegetables into bags, Red was getting pats and kisses. He figured out my local bookstore quickly, greeting shoppers as they came through the door, visiting the owner in her cubicle, finding a mat by the door to lie on. He loved to ride along with me to the gas station, the hardware store, even the dentist's office. He had never been on a leash and I never put him on one, either.

I am fortunate to live in Washington County, New York, a beautiful agricultural area where many people have animals and where dogs are as commonplace in the hardware store as they are in backyards. Red was eagerly adopted in my small town of Cambridge; there was almost no place where he was not welcomed.

When I took Red to a book reading at a local library, he went from row to row, as if he had done it a thousand times, greeting every person in attendance, and then came up to me, curled up into a ball, and went to sleep.

It occurred to me that there were so many boundaries around where Simon could go, and so few around Red. Simon's life was lived entirely within the pasture fence except for the walks we took up and down the road and into the woods. He loved people just as much as Red did, but our culture makes no allowances for animals like donkeys to be a part of our world, even though they would adapt easily to farmers markets, downtown parks, and school playgrounds. It was never going to happen. People did not cuddle up with donkeys; they are so large and most people are a bit afraid of them. Simon would often approach people who came to see him and seemed puzzled when they backed away or treated him gingerly, as if he might explode.

But Red opened a number of new windows on mercy and compassion for me. For one thing, he needed a lot of calm understanding before he could acclimate himself to my world. It took me less than a week to housebreak him. I put mats and carpets down on the floors until he could get used to smooth surfaces, I made sure I was giving him herding commands that he understood, and I lavished him with praise and attention when he got it right, which he invariably did.

I called a nursing home in Granville, New York, where Izzy and I had done some hospice volunteer work. I told them a little about Red, and they said they would love to have him visit the home. We went a few days later. We walked through the doors and right up to a woman in a wheelchair. She was astonished and delighted to see Red. She called him "Charlie," and he approached her and put his head on her knee as she patted him. The smile on her face was worth the trip, and I saw that Red had the same gift as Izzy — he could enter any space and be gentle and appropriate. You might have thought he had been doing it for most of his life, even though he had never been in a nursing home or any building like it. Mostly, he just wanted to be with me.

Dr. Thompson was right. Red was meant to be my dog, just as Simon seemed destined to be my donkey. It felt from the first as if I had lived with him for years. He became instantly popular. He had girlfriends everywhere — Lyle at the hardware store, Karen at the farm stand, Connie at the bookstore, Dawn at the dentist's office. They all kept treats for him and greeted him with great affection and enthusiasm. Soon, the dog that had never been inside of a building was inside a lot of them, every day.

And he had sheep right out the back door and got to work every day. He needed us, and we needed him, too. We had to move the sheep two or three times a day, keep them away from the donkeys' feeders, and get them inside the barn for visits from the vet. Red did the job.

The only cloud on the horizon, ironically enough, was Simon. He did not like dogs; he had not liked Rose, and he did not like Red. Donkeys are guard animals, and they see dogs as no different than coyotes. When Red came into the pasture, Simon's ears would go down, and he would lower his head to charge. Red, whose concentration when he was around sheep was laserlike, did not even notice or glance at him. That made me nervous. The first few times Red entered the pasture, I would stand between them, hold up my hand in front of Simon, and just say "Stop." Thankfully he did.

Ken Norman, our farrier, said it was almost impossible to trim Simon's hooves unless I was there. If I was, Simon would stand calmly while Ken did his work. Simon listened to me, and he obeyed me generally, and so did Red. Because I could control the two of them, I kept them apart and kept Red safe.

Red's Tao is different than Simon's or Rocky's. He is hardwired into me, responsive, and anticipatory; his life revolves around me. If I were thinking in mythological terms, Red would be the center animal. Simon and Rocky each lived in their own worlds of which we were part, but we were not the center of their universes.

Horses and donkeys are domesticated, but only somewhat. There is a part of them they keep to themselves, unlike dogs, who generally turn themselves over to us completely. Donkeys and horses have no desire to sleep on the edge of our beds or lie by our feet when we read. They live outside of our lives, not in the center. Red came into the center; he completed the circle in many ways. He filled in the blanks between what a dog does and what kinds of things other animals can do.

Simon spoke to me of the timeless ways in which animals like donkeys and human beings have always connected. Donkeys may work hard for humans, and ponies may keep them company and take them on rides, but dogs can wrap themselves right around your heart and soul. They live to serve. I came to love these animals in different ways, as they loved me in different ways.

FIFTEEN:
NEW BEDLAM FARM

Florence Walrath died at the end of 2011 at age 103, in her own bed in the house that she had loved and lived in for seventy-seven years. I did not get to know her as well as I would have liked, apart from hearing many legendary stories about her iron will, love of work, and passion for riding and swimming. That she had taken up water-skiing at age sixty was only one example of her refusal to let age define or confine her.

They took her driver's license away near the end because she couldn't see, and when they did that, she rode her mower up Route 22 to the lake so she could still swim. Then they took the mower away from her, too.

At the American Legion, to which her husband had belonged, the members kept an eye on her. They stopped by Florence's house to offer help in caring for the grounds and other chores. She always said no, she was fine, but on weekends, some of the members would just show up and mow her lawn when they saw that the grass was getting too high.

By the time I met Rocky, most of the fences around his pasture had disintegrated or just fallen down, and he could have trotted out onto the busy road in the front of the house and gone anywhere. Like Florence, he wouldn't think of it. The two of them, as she had predicted, were riding it out together.

With Florence gone, the family talked about Rocky's future. They couldn't bear to put him down. Florence loved him too much, and they knew that moving a blind old pony would be cruel, too much for him to bear.

So somebody came by every day to toss out some hay and grain. There was a swampy marsh out behind Rocky's pasture and a stream that ran all year. Rocky was on his own for water. Sometimes in the summer, the marsh would dry up for a day or two, but it would always fill up eventually.

Rocky was now more alone than ever. I have no reason to think that he minded being alone, although I am certain he noticed Florence's absence. How could he not have? I felt so bad for him, alone in this way, without his beloved human or any other animals to keep him company.

The interesting thing, when I thought about it, was that Rocky was a fortunate pony. In the wild, he would have been long dead by now, starved because he was unable to see to find food or torn apart by predators. He had been much loved and cared for in his life, and I knew that the most merciful thing would be for him to be left alone to live out his time in a place that was familiar to him. He was in so many ways the strongest and healthiest animal that I knew.

Rocky's routine never seemed to vary much. In the morning, he would come around to the side of the house and eat the grass and clover there. When the sun got strong, he got himself into the shade of the standing barn. In the afternoon, he would follow his trail back to the stream, drink some water, and graze by the brush.

Then, at night, he would stand by the back of the barn and wait for morning. When it rained or snowed, the overhang of the barn provided some shelter. Sometimes, when Maria and I visited, he would be covered in snow, as he would have been in the wild. He did not seem to mind.

We asked the family if it would be okay

for us to help take care of Rocky, and they said they would be pleased. With Florence's death and other issues, they had a lot on their hands.

For a time, I thought about moving Rocky to Bedlam Farm. I liked the idea of him and Simon together, two symbols of mercy and compassion, each in his own way. I imagined the donkeys looking out for Rocky — helping to guide him around the pasture. I imagined his pleasure at having a herd again.

I had some friends who had horses, and they talked me out of that plan. It would be traumatic for a blind animal that age to move. The stress of the move, of having to adjust to new terrain, could kill him. However, they all agreed that he would probably love being with the donkeys. Horses, like donkeys and sheep, like being with their own kind.

Maria and I had been married just two years when I first met Rocky, and we had been reconsidering our new lives together. Bedlam Farm is an idyllic place, the 1861 farmhouse sitting astride a hill overlooking the town of West Hebron. It has beautiful views, ninety acres of pasture and woods, and a mile-long path into the woods for us to walk with the dogs. It is a kind of paradise. The four old barns have been restored, and we put in a small screened-in porch with a sweeping view of the valley.

Yet we both felt it was time to move. There were a number of things to consider. Publishing had changed, and my income was less predictable. And Bedlam Farm had been my place; I bought it before I knew Maria and had lived there, mostly alone, for six years. We both wanted a place that would be ours together, and I knew that she would love a house that she could help choose and that we would make our home together.

We both wanted a farm, a place that would be good for the donkeys, dogs, sheep, and barn cats. Maria would need a studio outside of the house to work in. I would need a room in the house for my office. We'd also need a pen for the dogs, and a standing barn for hay and storage.

But we didn't need ninety acres. There were no longer cows or goats on the farm. I had reduced the herd of sheep from thirty-six to five; Maria sold the wool. Neither of us hunted or rode horses or was looking for more animals. We wanted a quieter, more manageable life. We put Bedlam Farm on the market and began looking around. I thought the farm would sell quickly. It did not. I thought we would find another home quickly. We did not.

Every place we looked at had a problem for us. There was a bad well in one. Another was on a floodplain. A third was isolated deep in the woods. A fourth didn't have an outbuilding where Maria could have her studio. We realized that what we thought would be a quick transition would be a long haul.

Rocky had altered the routines and rhythms of both of our lives. We had our own animals to care for, our own dogs to walk, our own work to do. But we both loved Rocky, were drawn into the life of this animal who seemed a mystic to me, so content by himself in his pasture.

Every afternoon, we found ourselves driving the thirteen miles to Florence's farm. The house was quiet, empty now, though Florence's collection of blue glass pieces still adorned the windowsills facing the pasture. Her spirit was very much in evidence.

When we pulled in, we would hear Rocky's gentle neigh, and no matter where he was, he would soon make his way to the back of the barn. We would enter from the front of the barn, open a sliding door, and walk down a concrete walkway. There was a gate, the top half open to the rear, and we would see Rocky's head bobbing. He would be waiting for us.

Rocky had a keen sense of where everything was, and when we put out his grain bucket, he would follow his nose to it, and this became the routine. First, his grain. Then we would open the gate and go outside. Maria would take out the brush we had brought. She would talk to him, sing to him, and sometimes give him an apple. Maria would pick the burrs out of his mane. This made him skittish at first, but he put up with it and stood still for it. After a few months, he would whinny when he felt the brush and slide over to Maria. Like donkeys, horses love to be groomed.

Maria was thorough, pulling out all of the knots in Rocky's hair, brushing the matted coat along his side and back. At first, his hair came off in large tufts, hairballs that would blow across the pasture. But after a while, his coat looked shiny and clean. When it snowed or there were ice storms, we would go over to the farm and brush Rocky off and give him some extra grain.

At those times, we wished he were with us, or we were with him. We wished he had shelter, and it was hard to leave him out in the cold. This is a human idea about compassion, I knew. Horses once lived in the wild, and Appaloosas have long, thick coats. Just because it was hard for us didn't mean it was hard for him.

A year passed and we became more attached to Rocky, and he to us. I thought it was time for Red to meet Rocky. We had been warned in the past that Rocky had an aggressive streak — that he was a biter and could turn hostile when surprised. So I wanted to be careful.

I took Red with me on a warm sunny day over to the Walrath farm. I approached the pasture gate calling out for Rocky as I always did to give him a chance to locate my voice and get used to it. "Hey, Rocky, it's me, Jon. How are you doing? What's going on?" That afternoon I told him I had a dog with me.

One of the many great things about Red is that you can totally trust him. If you tell him to stay, he will stay, and he will be staying in the same spot the next morning if you don't release him.

I heard Rocky's whinny when I opened the gate, and I called Red in. I put him in a lie down/stay and stood a few feet in front of him. I didn't want him to move, but I suspected Rocky would figure out soon enough that he was there.

I saw Rocky making his way up the gently

sloping pasture. He broke into a trot as he came near; he knew there was likely to be an apple. Red's ears went up as Rocky approached, but he didn't visibly react in any other way, as I knew he wouldn't. There had been a horse or two at the farm in Virginia where Red was before he came to me, so he wasn't shocked by Rocky's presence. He didn't seem to be shocked by anything much.

When Rocky got about ten feet from me he froze — I suspect he got wind of Red. He stopped and cocked his head. I could only imagine what the world seemed like to a blind old Appaloosa who had been in a pasture alone for more than a decade. There must have been all kinds of smells and sounds for him to interpret. For a new animal to be in the pasture so close must have seemed dangerous to him.

For several minutes he just raised his nose and sniffed. I kept talking to him to reassure him, holding out the apple. I took a few steps closer and so did he, and it took about fifteen minutes for us to get within arm's length of each other. Rocky eventually took the apple and worked it over carefully, raising his nose every few seconds to locate Red.

I called Red forward a few feet and had him lie down again. Rocky came close.

Soon, Rocky was almost on top of Red, and very carefully, he put his nose down on Red's back.

Red didn't move, and I was impressed and astonished by this. His ears went down, a sign of caution, but he never moved his body an inch, never growled, barked, or startled Rocky. The old pony ran his nose over every inch of him, and then he seemed satisfied.

I took a deep breath. It was a beautiful thing to watch, and Red seemed to be signaling Rocky that he was not a threat and would not be bothering him.

I released Red and he got up. And then I saw the strangest and most wonderful thing.

Red walked about ten feet toward the barn. Rocky put his nose up to locate Red and tilted his ears, perhaps to listen for the dog's breathing.

Red sat still, watching Rocky. Rocky walked over to Red, found him, and stood still. The two of them sat there like that for a few minutes.

Then Red got up and moved closer to the back of the barn, where I always fed Rocky his grain. This was a tricky path for Rocky. It led around old tires and brush, and I had seen him bump into the piles of old farm junk more than once. Red sat up, looking out at the field, and Rocky made his way over to the dog.

Then Red moved again right to the back of the barn door where Rocky got his grain. Rocky listened to hear where Red was going, sniffed the air, and then walked over to where the dog was sitting.

Red's demeanor was completely different than it was with the donkeys or sheep. He was completely calm, not vigilant or alert, as he was around Simon.

And then it hit me. Red knew Rocky was blind. I don't know how he knew, but it was clear that he knew. Perhaps it was the way Rocky sniffed or moved so carefully, perhaps it was the tentative way he walked. But it seemed to me that Red was guiding him to the back of the barn.

I was very much surprised by what I was seeing, although I had heard stories about dogs acting as guides for old and sick animals like horses. I'd had border collies for years. I'd never seen one who paid much attention to equines or animals other than sheep.

People love to project noble human motives onto dogs and other animals, but it seems an emotional response to me, not a considered one. Animals in my experience do not have motives beyond instincts and survival. They are neither "good" or "bad" in the way so many people seem to need to see them. Animals are not philosophers, they don't have narratives and language, and they can't consider their responses in the way human beings can.

My therapy dogs do not get up in the morning and choose to do good that day. They simply respond to attention and need — they smell and sense it and react to guidance, reinforcement, and reward. I have seen generosity in some dogs and other animals. Some will share food and some will not, but then again, instinct and other factors — such as the presence of siblings in infancy, the attentiveness of the mother, the availability of food, and human treatment — all shape the behavior of animals. None of an animal's responses has to do with conscious reasoning as much as genetics and learned behaviors.

Red was clearly a generous and tolerant dog, confident, calm, and secure. Rocky was a solitary blind animal suddenly in the company of another animal. Red had no fear of the pony, and Rocky came to trust this strange dog who had suddenly entered his life.

So this became a daily ritual for the two of them: Rocky approaching Red, Red standing still, then moving forward, Rocky coming up behind him. Red seemed to sense where Rocky needed to go — sometimes the pole barn, sometimes the outer pasture — and he would lead him there.

Was this how animals showed compassion for one another? Border collies like Red have among the most finely honed instincts in the animal world. I never saw him show a shred of compassion to a sheep who didn't move quickly or obey him instantly.

I believe compassion among animals is unpredictable and instinctive. Red did not experience Rocky as a sheep to be ordered around, and Rocky approached Red calmly. I thought that what I saw happening was Rocky teaching Red to be his guide dog, reinforcing behavior in a dog who loved ritualized and regular work. Red loves working and loves herding, and is eager for any task on the farm.

I think Rocky gave him one.

Animals of different species rarely interact with one another in ways we might call compassionate, but I had witnessed something remarkable. Something was going on between Red and Rocky. They had connected in the curious way animals sometimes do without talking or drama or declaration.

They simply accepted and seemed to recognize each other. Both animals were intuitive. Red was sensitive to other animals in the way working and herding dogs almost always are. And Rocky had developed powerful radar for friends and enemies — a blind pony living alone outdoors has to. Red sensed that Rocky was infirm. Rocky sensed that Red could help him navigate his dark world.

With each visit, this very touching relationship deepened. Red would take up a position leading to wherever Rocky wanted to go — the barn, the stream, the outer pasture. Red would sit and wait for Rocky to come up and locate him. Once Rocky was on his way and no longer needed his assistance, Red would turn and come back to me, like a bus driver who has made his final stop.

We'd watch Rocky follow a well-worn path to a corner of the north pasture where he spent much of the day, rain or shine. On the way back, he had to navigate around the collapsed barn, some tires and auto parts, and ditches, rocks, and mounds of dirt. When Red was there, Rocky would sniff until he found him — he always seemed to sense or know when the dog was present. He would touch Red's back with his nose and then Red would move five or ten yards toward the barn or the water trough.

In this way, he would lead Rocky back to the spots he knew well, and where he could always find his bearing. At first, I wasn't entirely convinced that this was happening, but it happened day after day, time after time. When we put grain out for Rocky, Red would sit within a few feet of it and stand by or lie down until Rocky was finished eating. We saw it so many times there was really no question about what was happening.

Rocky had a Seeing Eye dog.

One day our real estate agent Kristin Preble called up to talk about the sale of Bedlam Farm. "I don't know if you know this yet, but Florence Walrath's house is going on the market in a few months. I know the family would love it if you and Maria lived there. I just wanted to mention it to you."

When I told Maria about the phone call we looked at each other and both rushed over to the house. We walked the property, peeking in windows, and saw the same things. A big parlor inside the farmhouse that would be perfect for a study for me. A former one-room schoolhouse out back that had been hauled to the farm as a workshop for Florence's husband, Harold. It would need some work, but would be a great studio for Maria. And the surviving barn was in good shape; a lawn mower and some hay and feed could be stored there.

The farm had seventeen acres, enough land so we could walk around in the woods on our own property, but not too large for us to handle. And it was near Cambridge, a small town we both loved with a food co-op, a diner, and a great bookstore. The farmhouse had been built in 1849 and still had its original wonderful woodwork, as well as big, airy rooms. It was perfect for us.

Standing by the side of the house in that moment, I understood why I had stopped to photograph Rocky so long ago. He had called me to the farm, drawn me there. A magical helper, doing his work.

We called Kristin the next morning and told her we were interested. The first thing she said was what about the pony? If we reached an agreement on the house, would we keep him?

Of course, we'll take him as well, we said. Of course we would.

He was the reason we were coming to live there.

SIXTEEN:
THE TRIAD

When we decided to sell Bedlam Farm, we had three donkeys, two barn cats, two hens and a rooster, three dogs, and a part-time pony. Three of these animals — Simon, Red, and Rocky — converged on my life at the same time and were particularly powerful creatures. I often felt I was living in the middle of this almost mystical triangle. These three animals were connected to one another in ways that would further challenge and deepen my ideas about mercy and compassion. Together they taught me so much about how animals can heal and change a human being — me.

All of my time on Bedlam Farm, all of my dogs, all of my experiences — lambing, sickness, loss, sorrow — had led me to Simon, and he had led me further along the path. The paths we were walking were not really metaphorical at all; they turned out to be quite literal experiences.

If not for Simon, I would never have been open to Rocky. If not for Simon, I would never have been open to a stranger e-mailing me and telling me that God wanted me to have a border collie from Ireland in search of the right home. And for almost all of my life, I would have laughed at the idea that I would want a blind thirty-three-year-old Appaloosa pony.

However, I was no longer simply acquiring animals because I had the space, or because something in me was using animals to work out issues best dealt with in other ways. These were considered decisions. I felt as if these three animals came to me for particular and important reasons. And all of them had to do with my idea of grace — of living a more compassionate, considered, and meaningful life.

Simon continued to settle into the life of the farm. In most ways, he was now the dominant presence there. Before him, it had been Rose, the no-nonsense border collie who ran a tight ship and watched my back.

Simon was the largest animal on the farm, and as his body healed and he attached to us, he became a charismatic presence. He was not only the biggest animal; he made the most noise. His bray was getting louder and more raucous by the day and could be heard for miles down in the valley.

He was a celebrity now, in his own right. For years, people would come to the farm seeking a glimpse of the dogs, hoping for a photo with them. Now they were looking for Simon.

One day, he and I were walking down the road when a minivan with Pennsylvania plates pulled up. Tourists, I guessed. A woman rolled down the window and stuck her head out. "We're looking for Bedlam Farm, and we're lost. Can you help us?" I thought she was kidding at first. I was standing in the road with a donkey, but she was seriously lost.

I pointed up the road at my big barns and began to tell her who I was when one of the women behind the driver suddenly screamed, "Simon! That's Simon!" The doors slid open and five or six women with point-and-shoot cameras hopped out and started taking photos of Simon, who was soaking it all up, happy to be scratched, petted, and fussed over.

After they got all of their photos, they jumped back into the van and announced they were heading to nearby Manchester, Vermont, to do some outlet shopping.

"Oh," said the driver, waving from the window, "we love you too, Jon." Thanks, I said, amused, and Simon and I walked down to the waterfall at the bottom of the hill.

Rocky had entered my life in a different way. I felt he had summoned me. I knew the reason now, or at least part of the reason: to meet Florence Walrath and to find our new home. He was taking care of her beyond her death, settling her estate. Florence wanted someone to buy her home who would keep it mostly as it was and fix it up a bit. Rocky made it happen.

He also brought Maria and me to something we both wanted — a place to make a home together. Rocky also taught me about communicating — how to talk to a blind animal, how to listen to one. If the donkeys were intuitive, Rocky seemed mystical to me, sometimes literally coming right out of the mist to make his way to the gate, guided by my voice.

And then Red. Red is the dog I have been waiting for my whole life, and I have had wonderful dogs. He and I just fit like hand and glove. Red is never far from my side. When I go to a morning meditation gathering in my small town, he clambers up the stairs with me, greeting the meditators. He lies down when the first bell sounds and doesn't move until the final one rings. When

I sleep, he is at the foot of my bed. When I write, he is lying by my feet. When I am cooking in the kitchen, he is waiting by the door. He goes with me on the morning chores, gathers the sheep, and keeps them away from me while I take hay to the feeder.

He had entered my life through the powerful portal of the human-animal bond. A dozen times a day, I look at him and smile, in the way of people who love their dogs and who are lifted up by them.

There is always a reason why somebody loves one dog over another, why some would only get a rescued pit bull and others never would. Why some want a small dog and others a large one, some a mutt, others show dogs. There were reasons I had a neglected donkey, a beat-up border collie, and a blind Appaloosa pony in my life. Each had affected me. Simon broke loose some long-buried emotions in me, triggering a series of openings that spread into my life far beyond him. Rocky appeared to guide us to a new chapter in our lives, and taught me fresh lessons in mercy and compassion. And in Red there came the lifetime dog, the spirit dog, the dog to walk me through life, cheer me on, work with me, and inspire me in so many ways.

With three such animals, anyone's psyche,

emotional construction, and innermost feelings were bound to change. Because of them, I met all kinds of people. I was herding sheep again, greeting visitors in the barn, sharing images of them with people all over the world.

This was a powerful triangle, and I was right in the middle of it. In the following weeks and months I would come to see clearly that these three animals were, in fact, connected to one another, and all three of them were connected to me.

I have long studied the human-animal bond. I wrote a book about it, *The New Work of Dogs,* and spent some time at the University of Kentucky talking with attachment theorists. I've read the pioneering work on animal fantasies and attachments from Dorothy Burlingham and Anna Freud and followed the writings of John Bowlby on the ways in which infants do or don't attach to their families and to other living things.

I know that our feelings about animals are deeply woven into our own emotional histories. It is hard for human beings to look back into our own lives to understand why we love the animals we do. Animals are mirrors of our own psyches and emotions; they are reflections of our needs, wants, and experiences. There is a reason we think animals are cute, trustworthy, or unconditionally loving. I have learned that if you watch a woman on a horse, a man with his dog, or the passionate people of animal rescue, you are watching mirrored reflections, psychological videos if you will, of each human being's own potpourri of emotions — how they were treated in their earliest years, stories of nurturing, of soothing, of connection both good and bad. Our relationships with animals are reflections of us.

I have known this for some time, and in my own life, I understand that when I am speaking to an animal like Simon and decide to tell him about something so critically important and seminal as the death of my mother, then something is happening that has little or nothing to do with the animal, except perhaps that individuals like me sometimes trust them more than people.

My mother was a complex woman — not, I have come to see, unlike her youngest son, me. She was creative, anxious, restless, and manipulative. She was, she felt, defeated in her many ambitions by hostile or unsupportive men, including her husband, my father.

My mother always wanted more than she had, always wished for a different life. She ran a classy gift shop in Providence, an art gallery in Atlantic City during our brief time there, and was hostess of a vegetarian restaurant near Brown University back in Providence toward the end of her life. My mother always wanted to dance, to dress up and kick up her heels, but was married to a man who never wanted to dance or kick up his heels. They just didn't belong together.

She took out her frustrations and loneliness on her children, especially my sister and me, and we've spent much of our lives recovering. I loved my mother dearly and she loved me, but her relentless hostility, neediness, and many demands made it impossible for me to be near her for much of her life. She never saw any of the homes I lived in, and I would not let her anywhere near my daughter.

I mention this not to belabor my difficult childhood or to get even with her. I know she did the best she could and she gave me every one of the gifts that I have in life, including my love of storytelling, which she encouraged in me every day. But if there was a reason I was talking to a donkey on a country path in upstate New York, opening my heart up to him as I related one of the deepest wounds in my life, it was her.

People who struggled for connection with their mothers are the most likely to turn to animals for unconditional love and connection. Animals are safe and constant, and because they are dependent and can't speak, they are empty vessels, containers into which we can pour anything we wish.

This is where nurturing, memory, and need all collide. With Simon, I could be a mother and a brother. I could do for him what I wished had been done for me. I could give the very things I had needed and wanted so badly.

On one of our evening walks, I began to tell Simon the story of my mother's death. She had fallen on the floor of the bathroom in a residence for the elderly and was found in the morning when she did not appear for breakfast. They say someone filled her casket with flowers, a stranger. I didn't realize it at the time, but I had never told that story to anyone, not even Maria. I had never even permitted myself to think about it. My mother traded in guilt, that was her currency, and I could never think of her death without being nearly overwhelmed by it. Had I known she was dying, I would have rushed to see her, and I will always regret that I did not.

I am sorry to tell you, Simon, I said, that I did not see her for some years before her death, did not even know where she was. No one in my family called to tell me. Perhaps they thought I didn't want to know or would not care.

Simon was listening to me carefully. I could see his big ears swivel toward me, his round brown eyes looking at me. With Simon, I never feel he understands the words, but I always feel he knows what I mean. And when I am with him, I can say things I can't say to any human being. It just wouldn't come out right.

My mother was a beautiful woman, Simon, and she loved me very much. She taught me to tell stories, and she laughed at them and convinced me that they were wonderful. After she died, they sent me a scrapbook she kept filled with stories and photos and clippings of me and my work.

I found myself on the path telling Simon the story of my mother, and as it came out, I realized I was finally coming to terms with feelings I had never spoken out loud.

My mother's dreams ended when she lost her hostess job, when the owner, her dear friend, died of cancer. After that, she lost her iron will and finally surrendered to the strong tides of life.

It was like that for her. She kept breaking out and the world kept rounding her up and sending her back to jail. It drove her mad, Simon, made her crazy and angry and hurtful, and I could not be around her at the end of her life. I wish I could have been. I loved her dearly, but I couldn't. People are like that: they make these decisions for all kinds of reasons they don't always understand. Their lives are not instinctive and orderly like donkeys' lives. I am sorry I did not get to say good-bye to her, Simon. A man should say good-bye to his mother.

Of course, Simon neither understood the story of my mother nor cared about it. I admire donkeys and respect their intuitiveness, but animals do not, I believe, relate to this very human world of emotions — do not waste their time on guilt, regret, envy, or hurt. This was all about me. What was important about it, what was significant, though, is that Simon did bring it out of me, did get me to tell it, to speak it out loud, to consider it.

I realized after our walk that I had work to do. Two weeks later, Maria and I drove to Providence. We found the cemetery where my mother and father are buried and on a cold, bright winter day, we found the grave markers.

Life is ironic. My mother and father were almost never together in life, but there they were, side by side, together for all time. Maria stood with me, then left me alone.

"Hey, Mom," I said. "I want you to know that I am sorry about us. I love you very much and I know you love me. I forgive you for anything that needs to be forgiven. I have found someone to love and am very happy. I just want you to know that and to say that I'm grateful for the many gifts you gave me. I wish you had been happier in your life, but that was never up to me."

I felt as if a poisonous cloud had left me and was swept by the wind through the old Jewish cemetery and away. Wow, I told Maria, I see what they mean about donkeys. Look what they can do for you.

Did Simon want to help me forgive my mother and move on — something that was decades overdue? No, I think not. Did he sense there was some feeling inside of me that needed to come out? Did he smell it and feel it instinctively? Yes, I believe he did, and if I had done him a great service in bringing him to my farm, he more than returned the favor.

Because, I asked myself, if I could feel mercy and compassion for this beat-up donkey, why couldn't I feel it for my own mother, who fought desperately for a meaningful life and simply could not figure out how to find one? In her bitterness and rage, she hurt a lot of people, and a lot of people, including me, hurt her back. If I couldn't feel compassion for her, then what did that really say about me?

When an animal guides you, emotionally and spiritually, it is not an obvious thing. Rather, they open doors indirectly, and then a domino effect sets in. They open up one part, and that experience opens up another. This was, in many ways, the lesson of Simon, his legacy.

Seventeen:
The Move

We bought Florence's farm and were committed to moving into our new home by Halloween of 2012. I've moved a lot in my life, always hiring movers. They'd come to the house, stuff everything in big cartons, and then unstuff them when we got to the new house.

That was a long time ago, another world. We had little money to put toward the move, but our friend and carpenter Ben Osterhaudt, who did so much work on both Bedlam Farm and our new farm, said he would get a buddy with a trailer and move us in an afternoon. In the meantime, Maria and I began the first of what seemed like a thousand trips hauling stuff to our new home in our Toyota Highlander.

The new house was much more intimate than Bedlam Farm: spare, less grand, but beautiful in its own way. We couldn't take but half of our stuff.

We talked about many things while we prepared for the move, but we were especially excited at the thought of Simon, Rocky, and Red living together on the same farm. With Lulu and Fanny there also, and Maria's small herd of sheep, Rocky would finally have his herd, Simon and Lulu and Fanny their permanent homes. Red would have the life he deserved, and Rocky would have his Seeing Eye dog.

Simon would have an equine buddy. We both loved the image. When you come out of a tough and painful divorce, as Maria and I both had, your sense of family is shattered. The animals were healing for both of us, and the idea of our moving and reforming in this cozy new peaceable kingdom was very much in our heads.

We researched the animal move and planned it like a space launch. Ken Norman, our farrier, would move the animals. The donkeys first, then the sheep. It is not so simple to move donkeys where they don't want to go, and none of our donkeys thought getting in a trailer was a good thing. We had done it once with Lulu and Fanny, and they almost took the barn — and the trailer — apart. Ken was big and strong and would throw a rope behind their rear legs and pull. Once he got them near the trailer, he would simply get behind them and shove.

At our new farm, we had Ben build a pole barn right off the big barn. It was a cost-effective way to shore up the big barn and provide shade and shelter for the animals. The barn was cleared out, so now there was a stall available to house Rocky in bad weather. We built a skip barn — a portable sheep barn that could be moved back and forth — in the sheep pasture. We ordered two hundred bales of hay from Nelson Green, considered the best hay maker in the county.

I ordered two heated hoses. Our budget didn't allow for a frost-free pump right then, so I hatched an elaborate plan to install an outdoor frost-free faucet, attach it to the heated hose, and run it outside to the barn behind the farmhouse.

We hired a tractor to clear the brush and some other workers to clear the pasture of debris. We ordered two truckloads of gravel for the feeding area by the barn.

We also talked to two large-animal vets, some farriers, and several friends with horses to ask them how we could best ac-climate the donkeys with Rocky. Rocky's blindness meant he couldn't really defend himself from the usual jockeying, bumping, and biting that went along with equine introductions.

Just about everyone told us the same thing, and it squared with our own sensibilities. Separate Rocky and the donkeys for a few days; let them become aware of one another. And then introduce them, leaving them together for short periods of time.

The advice was unanimous: they would work it out. Animals always work it out. The donkeys would sense that Rocky was old and infirm — would see that he was no threat.

And to be honest, this was also my experience. Animals don't feud or make war; they survive and adapt. And why wouldn't they work it out? An old blind pony is no threat to healthy donkeys and sheep. As always, they would take their cues from us. Maria and I always set the tone on Bedlam Farm. Everybody gets fed, everybody has shelter, everybody gets fresh water and lots of attention. The animals in my life have little to envy and no reason to squabble; they all get what they need.

Animals always act in their self-interests, not out of emotional motives. Donkeys are companion animals for many horses, and I've often seen them out grazing together. The farm was compact, the pastures small. Maria and I were almost always on hand to keep an eye on things, to encourage the right behaviors, to reinforce the atmosphere of our farm. It was a peaceable kingdom. It would stay that way.

We moved the donkeys first. Ken came by with a friend and a small horse trailer. We backed it up to the barn. That morning, we had lured the donkeys into one of the barn stalls with some carrots.

Lulu, the watch-donkey of the group, the smartest and most vigilant, was not fooled. Fanny and Simon came running in for the treats. Lulu got to the door, took a look at me and Maria, and balked. But it was too late. Fanny and Simon were already inside munching on the grain we had put down in bowls. I got behind Lulu, smacked her on the butt, and slid the barn door closed. She had nowhere to go, but I could see that she sensed something was up.

Ken showed up with his trailer and backed it up to the barn door. By now, Fanny knew something was up as well, and she and Lulu tried nosing the barn door open. Simon, trusting as always, was hoping for another carrot.

We opened the barn door, put up gates to the back of the trailer, and got into the stall behind the donkeys. Lulu led the charge out, but there was nowhere to go except into the trailer. She tried to bust through the gates, but Ken was waiting for her. We put some grain in the trailer, banged some trash cans behind them, and Simon was the first one to jump in. Lulu and Fanny followed, as donkeys do. They were not going to be separated.

It took less than half an hour to drive the trailer over to the new farm. We had put Rocky in his stall inside the barn, separated by a gate.

When we got to the new place, we opened up the back of the trailer, and Simon was the first one out. All the donkeys looked a bit rattled from the drive, but curious about their surroundings.

Simon came walking quickly up to me, and I gave him a carrot, which he chewed gratefully. Lulu and Fanny weren't buying it yet and wouldn't take any food, but seeing Maria and me calmed them down. Rocky neighed in the barn, and all three donkeys were soon outside of the gate, sniffing the air and looking in. We left them to get used to the place. Later, when we left to go back to Bedlam Farm — we humans wouldn't be moving into the new house for a few days — the donkeys were out grazing in the field.

Like most animals, they did not waste a lot of time missing what they had left behind, not when there was fresh green grass. They checked Rocky out from time to time, but we were pleased by the first encounter. It seemed like no big deal. They would figure it out.

The move changed us both in ways we had not considered or really even imagined. Every day I did things I had never done before. Necessity is the mother of invention. And of self-reliance, as well. I learned how to steam wallpaper off of a wall, pry open jammed windows, stack firewood, putty holes in walls, polish and paint wood.

I was at the hardware store a half dozen times a day looking for glue, the right screwdriver or hammer, the right kind of nail. I got Florence's creaky forty-year-old mower repaired and kept my promise to mow my own lawn instead of paying someone else to do it, as I had for years.

Each day I talked to Ben about slate roofs and putting new windows in the barn to keep the snow out. I hauled debris from the pasture out to the woods and down to the dump.

Maria and I did most of these things together. She had once forsaken making art for a career in home restoration, and the last thing she wanted to do was spackle and paint, but she did, and I did, and because it was something we were doing together, because we were working on our new house together, we both loved doing it. Most nights, we collapsed into bed, filthy and exhausted, and were asleep before we could even turn the lights out.

I didn't realize how much we had needed to leave Bedlam Farm until we left. I was often asked, "How could you leave such a beautiful place?" Pride kept me from confessing at least part of the truth — we couldn't really afford the upkeep anymore. But the real reason was more difficult to explain. The scale of my life had changed. My values, too. I was finally running my own life responsibly, and I wanted to do some of the things that other men did, to learn to repair and build and care for the physical objects in my home and in my life. I was astonished at how much money we were saving doing so much work ourselves. It was something of a breakthrough when the toilet kept running and I started to call a plumber. Instead, I put the phone down, went to the hardware store and got a rubber stopper for the tank, and fixed it myself.

I began calling the new farm Bedlam Farm 2.0. It had all the qualities we loved about the old farm, but was scaled to fit to our current life. The grounds were smaller, the hay right upstairs in the barn, the water buckets fifty feet from the back door. The house was more compact and intimate. I had to be careful about cluttering it up — the old Bedlam Farm house was big and sprawling; it easily absorbed all of my junk, papers, books, and clothes. We no longer had a screened-in porch, and the old windows were rotten at the sills. When we opened them it was like a superhighway for bugs and flies. Still, we coped, and I dragged two Adirondack chairs out by the back pasture where we could sit and enjoy our beautiful new surroundings.

The move drew us even closer together; Maria loved having *our* house rather than us living in my house. She took ownership of the new place so differently and intensely. The new house was her "adorable place," as she put it.

We were now close to several towns, including Bennington, Vermont, and Cambridge, New York. Everything we needed was closer — gas stations, hardware store, friends, doctors. We lived a few hundred yards from Momma's restaurant, so we could walk down the road to get a burger or a wrap when we were hungry; we didn't have to drive thirty miles. I spent so much less time in cars.

Simon and I still enjoyed our daily chats. I offered the opinion that the new farm was a good place for both of us and he seemed to agree, watching me closely, chewing his carrot. He seemed as content as I was. He loved the new pole barn, and walking the flat pasture was much easier on his battered legs (and on mine).

We built a dog run behind the house, and the dogs settled in, as dogs will. Red had sheep in the backyard again, my Lab, Lenore, had a pasture to explore, and our guard dog, Frieda, had a lot of trucks to keep at bay.

We scrambled to fix up the old schoolhouse on our property to be Maria's studio. We needed help for this. Ben came and sanded and polished the floors. He poured insulation into the walls and fixed all the holes in the side. We put in track lighting and a baseboard heating system. Maria settled in to her new studio happily, cranked up her blog, and began making and selling her quilts and fabric art. I was happy, too. I took over the parlor where the pastor used to visit and set up my Apple computer. We got right to work.

The old Bedlam Farm had been remote, but our new home was close to friendly neighbors. One by one, they came over to welcome us, offer us help, and tell us the secrets of the neighborhood. And we began the exciting and draining process of entering a new community. I volunteered to teach a writing workshop at an arts center in town, while Maria volunteered to work at the town food co-op.

Our days were rich and full. We did our work, visited the animals, scrubbed cabinets, and repaired old lamps. At night, Maria and I would head out to the Adirondack chairs by the back pasture and hold hands and watch the moon rise in the sky.

"How does it feel?" I asked Maria one night after many hours of wallpaper scraping; there were bits of wallpaper down my back and in my hair. "It feels like home," she said. For me, too.

Eighteen:
Trouble in Paradise

Maria and I both like to remember that sunny fall day when Rocky took us for a walk in his secret garden. He had several spots — hiding places, perhaps safe places — which he would visit regularly, usually daily.

One of Rocky's regular haunts was the corner of the south pasture where clover grew. It was private and shrouded by old trees, bounded by a busy road. Another was below the apple tree behind the big barn, where he would often graze and stare out at the world, listening, perhaps remembering when he could see.

But I think Rocky's favorite spot was out of sight, down the hill behind the big barn, across a marshy stream. Sometimes, when we called him, he would be down there. Sometimes he would come out, sometimes not.

One beautiful Sunday afternoon, when we

finished brushing and grooming Rocky, he whinnied and pranced around us playfully. We had never seen him so exuberant before. Old as he was, Rocky usually moved slowly and deliberately. But this afternoon, buoyed by some time with Maria, his old spirit seemed to surface, and he turned his head down toward the bottom of the hill and then seemed to wait for us.

It was hard, sometimes, to separate love from compassion when it came to Rocky, but sometimes compassion can grow into love. When I first met Rocky, I just felt sorry for him, this old blind pony alone in his pasture for years, his human fading after a century of life. But as I got to know him, this feeling of being merciful deepened. I loved the way he and Maria connected. I admired his independence. He accepted. He endured. There was something wonderfully noble about Rocky — something heroically stoic — and I came to love him for that.

That morning, he trotted down the hill, turning several times to wait for Maria, Red, and me. We waded across the wet grass, pulling some wooden planks across the swampy water. The marsh was about ten feet across, and then a gentle hillside rose up. Rocky stood there until we caught up, and then turned to the right, to a path hidden from view up the hill at the barn.

A field opened up — a gentle pasture, surrounded by shrubs and brush and another stream. Rocky went over to the stream — we saw his hoofprints everywhere — and drank from it. He sniffed some of the wildflowers, nibbled on some berries, pulled up some deep green marsh grass. He came over and sniffed Red and whinnied, it seemed in great pleasure, time and again.

It was a golden memory, one of those connections between people and animals that bond us to them, and they to us. We walked all around Rocky's secret garden, a place that had given him comfort, safety, and food perhaps all of his life, a place tucked away out of the consciousness of any human. And he had shown it to us; he had brought us there, just as he had brought us to the farm.

To this day, Maria cries when she thinks of it.

I've learned a lot of things in my time on my farms, and perhaps the single biggest lesson is that my plans and hopes and expectations must be a source of great amusement to whatever forces govern the earth. The farm is a powerful teacher; life and death and crisis and mystery all happen almost daily.

We watched Rocky and the donkeys with some anxiety. We wanted things to work out. We loved these animals and expected to be with them a long time.

Caring for Rocky and keeping him on the farm was one of the most beautiful experiences Maria and I have ever known, and the fact that we could share it made it even more powerful. At first, he seemed to be living in a fog, but as he got to know me, and especially Maria, this changed. He seemed to be thriving. With his teeth fixed, he was eating more comfortably and keeping his weight up, something that was important for an aging pony. He moved more quickly, and sometimes even broke into a trot. One moonlit night I swear I saw Rocky dancing in the mist, out by the stream. He was so sweet and appealing.

Sometimes I would sit and watch him and Maria, as she sang to the pony, talking to him, brushing the burrs out of his coat, this long-neglected creature visibly soaking up the attention. He had someone loving him again, caring for him.

Everywhere we went in our new town, people asked how Rocky was doing and told us how great he was looking, all shiny and brushed. Many people remembered and loved Florence, and many others just loved to drive by and see the pony grazing quietly. Like Florence herself, Rocky was a symbol of other times.

Florence had once said that there was really no reason for either she or Rocky to still be alive; they were both just too tough to die. Florence's love of Rocky was perhaps one of the most merciful and compassionate things I had ever seen between a human and animal. It just touched my heart, and deeply.

Caring for Rocky became a part of our lives, our routine, the string of chores that connected Maria and me to the farm, to Simon and the other donkeys, and to the rest of the animals.

It was also a lot of work. Because Rocky had to be kept separate from the donkeys for a while, there was a lot of mucking to do in his stall. He got fresh hay twice a day and we hauled buckets of water in for him. He was also brushed regularly and given special high-calorie grain to put some weight on him for the winter.

We hadn't quite figured out yet how we would feed him in the winter. The donkeys would be eating in their hay feeder, and we couldn't expect a blind old pony to bump his way into that scrum.

At the end of two weeks, we were pleased with the acclimation process. Simon and Lulu and Fanny spent a lot of time outside of Rocky's stall, nosing the gate, sniffing him, staring at him. It seemed as if the herd was already forming. They all seemed to be together a lot of the time, even if separated by a gate. Simon just stared at Rocky sometimes, but otherwise didn't seem to know he was there.

So at the beginning of the third week, we opened the stall. Red was there, and he walked out with Rocky, who stopped, sniffed the air carefully, and then sniffed for Red.

It took him a few minutes, but he walked out of the pole barn entrance, found his path, and headed out to his pasture, out by the road and alongside the farmhouse. Simon and Lulu and Fanny were a few yards away, and all three of them stared at Rocky and seemed to freeze.

Rocky lifted his nose to sniff them and then trotted quickly down his path. He didn't seem to care about the donkeys; he just walked past them. Maria and I had decided to be present for the first week or so when Rocky was with the donkeys. We would either be right there watching or in a spot in the house where we could look out and see the pasture. This was relatively easy to do, as the pastures wrapped around three sides of the farmhouse. We decided to be cautious. Rocky would be out for only several hours a day, at first, until everyone could get used to one another. What we were told, what we expected to happen, was that there would be some tension, some curiosity, even some bumping and snorting before things settled down.

There were also gender dynamics to deal with, of course. Rocky was gelded, as was Simon, but males could be competitive around one another. They could also be protective of the females. Most of the people we talked to believed that donkeys were sensitive enough to grasp that Rocky was old and infirm. They would, after a while, have little interest in him.

For the first two weeks of the trial, Maria and I were back and forth in the pasture all day. After a couple of hours, we would bring an apple out, call Rocky, or send Red out to get him. He always followed Red and stayed close to him.

We were pleased with the results. All was going smoothly. Rocky got his exercise, visited his pasture and secret garden, and by afternoon he was back locked safely in his stall. Simon was always vigilant around Rocky, but that was natural for donkeys.

Our theories of animal care — animals with food, attention, and shelter have few reasons to quarrel — were working out. My triad of powerful new animal spirits — Rocky, Red, and Simon — was coming together and living together. Simon was reborn. Red was happy and busy. Rocky was no longer alone.

Here's the thing about hubris though: you can coast along on it for a good long while, but when you fall off the cliff, it's a long drop.

By the third week, we no longer felt it was necessary for us to be present. When Rocky was out in the pasture, he kept to his routine — the far pasture grazing in the morning, his secret meadow in the late afternoon. We were planning to keep him out in the outer pasture with the other animals at night, where he had always been, unless the weather was bad. Because of his age, we decided Rocky would have dibs on the stall in the barn if it was awful outside. The donkeys and sheep would have plenty of shelter in the pole barn.

One day I needed to go into town to pick up some groceries. As I was walking to the car, I sensed some movement out in the field and I turned. I saw Rocky walking slowly toward the barn. Beyond him, with his ears flat and his head down — the posture of the charging donkey — was Simon, bearing down on Rocky at full speed.

Red was not in the pasture. Rocky was staying on his familiar path. It was like watching a slow-motion horror film. I saw Simon moving toward the blind creature, and I shouted and ran, waving my arms, hoping to stop Simon or at least alert Rocky.

As I ran toward the gate, I saw Simon plow right into the pony, braying and snorting. He bit Rocky hard on the back, and with his great forward motion drove the pony off of his feet and directly into the electrified fence and fence posts behind him.

Rocky didn't know what had hit him, and I could hear the charge from the fence crackling and popping as he slammed into it, bounced off, and fell to the ground. Rocky's ears and tail were twitching. For a second I thought he had died of shock. Simon, ears still down, circled and began to charge again, just as I opened the gate and, waving my arms and shouting, ran between them.

It is never a wise thing to step between two large animals in conflict, but I didn't really think about it. The sight of Rocky, stunned, lying next to the fence, struggling to get his footing, was too much for me.

Screaming "Simon, Simon, stop!" I got in front of him before he got to Rocky again. Simon always pays attention to me, and I could not quite believe what I was seeing.

Simon stopped, looked at me, and backed up. I charged at him, shouting and flailing my arms. He turned and ran back to Lulu and Fanny, both standing about fifty yards back watching. He seemed shocked that I had yelled at him.

"I'm sorry, Rocky," I said, leaning down over the pony as he struggled to get up. Rocky got to his feet, and, panicked, turned and ran back down the pasture out to his corner of the field near the outer fence. I looked up and saw that Simon had circled around and was starting to pursue him there. I got in front of Simon and waved my arms again and drove him back.

Didn't Simon see that Rocky was old? Helpless? Blind? That he was no threat?

This was Rocky's home, after all. Simon was the interloper. Didn't Simon understand? My whole notion of him collapsed right there in the pasture. He was no longer the gentle Platero, walking with me on the path, musing about life. He was something very different.

Maria heard the shouting and came running into the pasture. I told her what had happened.

"Why?" she asked. "Why did Simon do that?"

I had no idea, I said. His aggression seemed to come out of the blue. We were completely unprepared for it.

It took us an hour to get the shocked and rattled pony out of the pasture. First I got the donkeys into the sheep pasture on the other side of the farmhouse and locked them in. Then we sent Red out to sit in front of Rocky and guide him back in. Red's presence seemed to settle Rocky. He grew calm enough that we could get close to him. We saw some bite marks on his back and hindquarters, but no blood. He seemed to be walking steadily enough.

I kept hearing the sound of him crashing into the fence — it was now bent back several feet — and the popping sound of his body hitting the wire. The fence on the farm hadn't been charged for years during Florence's time, so this was probably the first time Rocky felt a shock. Between Simon crashing into him and biting him, and him falling into the wire, I could only imagine how traumatized he was.

We got Rocky back into his stall and let

the donkeys back into the main pasture. Simon and the girls came right up to the stall and stood there, only this time I saw a different look on Simon's face. His ears were up, his eyes were wide, and he was snorting.

Ever since I adopted Simon, a rosy glow had surrounded my notions of animals. Rebirth and resurrection are powerful ideas, and I think animals make it possible to experience both time after time. And, of course, I was a hero. Everywhere I went, people thanked me for saving Simon, for taking him in, for giving the story of his rescue such a happy ending. And among animal people, happy endings are precious, much loved, valued, and shared.

But one thing more powerful than our love of animals is our love of self, and there is no story more gripping or enduring than the ones we like to tell about ourselves.

Simon had, in some ways, and from the first, stopped being a donkey and became a material manifestation of what I needed him to be: Platero, walking gently with me through life, a sweet, grateful, devoted creature, a lover of children, of work, of me.

It's amazing how the mind works, how you see and hear what you want to see and hear until something shocks you into seeing what you need to see. I called some friends, went online, and pulled some books on horses and donkeys off of the shelf.

This time, everything I saw pointed in a different direction and suggested a different outcome — a different ending that was not happy. Yes, sometimes it works out to introduce a new equine to a herd, but sometimes there is a tough period of acclimation. It is common for donkeys and horses to bite and kick newcomers. It is also quite common for a herd to reject an outsider, especially if he or she is injured or aged. In the wild, these newcomers would draw predators in and endanger the herd. The flock leaders would commonly attack and drive off a weak intruder to protect the herd. In addition, a male is much more likely to drive off a male intruder, even if he is healthy, as it threatens his dominance of the herd.

I was shocked reading this. It was precisely the opposite of what we had been hearing. Why hadn't I found it before? But it also made perfect sense. I called back all of the people whose advice I had sought, the ones who had said my donkeys and Rocky would work it out.

"Oh," said one when I described Simon's

assault on Rocky. "It will never work out. Simon is protecting his herd, his women. He'll never accept a blind old pony."

Another said sadly over the phone. "Can you find another home for Simon? That's the only way it can work. You can't move a blind old pony, and the donkeys will never accept him."

I couldn't quite believe what I was hearing. The same people who had been so confident about things working out were now telling me it would never work out.

I called a large-animal vet I knew and trusted, one who was experienced treating equines. "I'll be honest with you," she said. "Simon is doing his job. He is protecting his herd. He will not submit to a weak old male horse being around the females he is protecting. Rocky is old, tired. This is too much stress for him. He should not be subjected to another winter."

I asked the vet if she was saying I ought to euthanize Rocky.

"If he were mine, I would," she said. "I wouldn't subject him to another winter." Her words hit me like a bomb. My first thought, honestly, was of Maria. She had come to love Rocky dearly, he was her little pony.

So, I was confronted with compassion

again, that word, that idea. Compassion for Rocky, who had endured so much on his own, who had found so much again — Red, Maria, me, fresh grain, good hay, shelter from the rain, company, and purpose.

Compassion for Simon, who was protecting his herd, doing his job, driving off the danger.

Compassion for Maria, who loved her pony dearly, who had waited a long time to open herself up to the love of animals, and who was transformed every morning when she stood in the pasture brushing this pony, handing him slices of apples, who saw that Rocky was only too happy to accept the love of a human being again.

But what was compassion here, really? Was it keeping Rocky in this suddenly dangerous and difficult life? Or was it letting go? In the animal rescue world in our time, compassion is almost uniformly defined as keeping animals alive, at all costs, by any means.

Compassion on a farm, with real animals, is often very different. There is no such thing as a no-kill farm. I had learned the hard way that compassion sometimes means letting go, not hanging on. And there are no real guidelines to follow but your heart.

■ ■ ■ ■

While we tried to figure out what to do, we followed a course of watchful waiting, again keeping an eye on Rocky and the donkeys as they grazed. One afternoon, when the donkeys were grazing in one corner of the pasture and Rocky in another, I went into the house to get something to drink.

As I was coming out, Ben, our handyman who was working to repair the barn, called out that he had just seen Simon charge Rocky and drive him into the fence. Rocky was standing in a muddy part of the pasture that was filled with spring rain, a place he had run to get away from Simon. From some yards away I could see the bite marks on his back and saw Rocky trembling.

It is difficult, still, to describe what I felt for that poor old pony, living on his own, finding his own paths, his own secret garden, his life suddenly invaded by new people bringing new animals, and his peaceful gambol shattered by being attacked, bitten, and driven into fence posts and electrical wires. If any creature was entitled to some peace and quiet, some stability and security, it was Rocky.

I was furious. I felt nothing but rage for

Simon, and I rushed out into the pasture and saw him charging toward Rocky again. I ran as quickly as I could and intercepted him, swinging my hand out and slapping him hard on the side of his face.

I yelled at him, "Simon, what's the matter with you? After what you've been through, you would do this to him? How could you?"

I'm not sure who was more astonished at this, Simon or me. He screeched to a halt, his ears straight up, and he looked at me as if I had just fallen out of the sky, as if he did not know who I was, as if he could not believe it was me.

I felt just awful. My face flushed with shame, anger, and regret.

I had slapped him to stop him from slamming into Rocky again, but I had also struck him out of rage. It came from deep inside of me, from my darkest places.

Simon froze and just stood staring at me. I was horrified. I rushed over to him and hugged him and kissed him on the nose. I rubbed the spot where I had struck him. How quickly my own convictions about mercy and compassion had collapsed in a fury because Simon had behaved like a donkey instead of a human being, instead of me.

Rocky had vanished. Sensing Simon's approach, he must have turned around and trotted back for the safety of his watery marsh. The fence post was bent from his collision with it. He seemed to think he would be safe standing in the water, about five or six inches high. He seemed to know that the donkeys would not pursue him there.

I stood rubbing Simon's ears, talking to him. I have rarely felt so bad about my life with animals as I did at that moment, having struck Simon and seen Rocky nearly attacked.

A farmer I knew who lived near Bedlam Farm came by one day to ask me for a copy of a book I had written — *Going Home: Finding Peace When Pets Die* — because he had just lost his border collie. I knew how much he had loved that dog. He lived to be fourteen years old and was with the farmer every minute of every day, riding in the tractor, in his pickup, chasing his cows all over the field.

"How did he die?" I asked him.

"Oh," he said, "I shot him."

I blinked, and then asked why.

"Well, he was getting sicker by the day, and he couldn't get around much anymore and I could see he was in a lot of pain."

But, I said, curious, why shoot him? Why not take him to the vet?

"I wanted to be humane," he said. "It was better for me to kill him with one shot than for him to die on the floor of some vet's office."

Knowing how much this man loved his dog, I saw mercy in a completely different way. I remember thinking, this is pure compassion, direct and unfiltered. He was thinking of nothing but his dog.

The real world of real animals was not what many people wanted to see, perhaps myself included. This was another lesson that Simon had taught me. Real compassion is not easy — not as simple as loving a cute animal in need of a home. Real compassion, I came to see, involved empathy — the ability to set aside my own definition of goodness and put myself in the head of another living thing, in this case a donkey. Mercy often takes the form of self-righteousness in our world — you are bad because you didn't do what I would do; you are evil because you chose to end a life rather than preserve it at all costs.

Mercy and compassion involve self-respect. Both ask us to look in the mirror and be comfortable with our decisions, not ask others what they think of our decisions.

It is this idea, I think, that so often gets lost in the swirl of judgment and anger that shroud the very ideals of humanity.

That awful day when Rocky was attacked again, I walked over to Simon and handed him a cookie. I kissed him on the nose again and apologized, once again, for slugging him. "Thanks," I said, "for being a donkey. I'm slow to understand, but I'm getting there."

I called our vet about Simon's latest attack on Rocky, and I told her that I didn't think it was going to change, it wasn't going to end, they weren't going to work it out. Simon's protective instincts were very powerful and they weren't going to go away just because I demanded it or wanted it. I could see it in Simon's eyes, in the way he looked at Rocky, in his body language; I could sense it in him, just as he sensed things in me.

I described the attacks in detail. I also talked about my concerns for Rocky. He was clearly affected by the presence of the donkeys and the attacks. He was tense, sticking to the far corners of the pasture, staying out as long as he could. Winter was approaching. He was losing weight, getting frail.

"I have the feeling," I told the vet, "that

the most merciful thing to do would be to put Rocky down. This all seems to be unraveling him. I have the feeling that this is his time. Florence is gone; other animals are here. Rocky seems spent to me."

She was quiet for a minute or two, and then said: "Jon, Simon will not accept this pony. He is a clear danger to the herd in his eyes. Simon is just doing his job. You have to do yours. It's your decision."

The next morning, we got up earlier than usual, went out to the barn, put the donkeys out in the sheep pasture. We brought Rocky out to the pole barn. I stood silently while Maria brushed him, talked to him, sang to him. He leaned into her, almost gratefully.

Red came and lay down in front of him, waiting to guide him out into the pasture. Maria and I talked of the day when Rocky had taken us out for a walk in his secret garden, seemingly happy for the company, proud to show us around.

The vet came early, as she promised. Maria said her goodbyes to Rocky, told him she knew he was ready to go. I patted the old pony and said, "Thank you, Rocky, I know you are going to a better place, perhaps to meet Florence there." Rocky was given one injection in the neck. He fell instantly to the ground and was dead by the time the vet kneeled to put a stethoscope over his heart. Red came over and sniffed the body, then lay down next to it, looking out at the pasture.

The donkeys, normally so curious, were not curious about this. Out of sight, out of mind.

As the vet gathered her things to leave, she turned to me and said, "Thank you for being merciful to him." And it was over. Maria and I stood and held hands for a while. She said she didn't want to be there when the haulers came to take the body away.

Red and I waited for them. They came quickly.

Rocky was gone; my triad was dissolved. I had learned a few more things about Simon, and about mercy and compassion.

I walked over to the sheep pasture and let Simon and the donkeys out. To the best of my knowledge, Simon did not see what had happened. Yet he didn't even look at Rocky's stall or the pole barn where he had been glaring at the pony for days.

He seemed smaller, gentler. His ears were up; he moved more slowly and seemed at ease. He came right over to me and put his nose in my stomach, which is what he did when he wanted some attention.

"I'm sorry, Simon," I said. "You were just doing your job. You were just being your own kind of hero."

NINETEEN:
AFTERWARD

Rocky's death hit us hard, but a farm does not pause much for grieving and reflection. The animals have to be fed and watered, fences fixed, dogs walked. We have lost dogs, chickens, sheep, cows, and donkeys in our time on farms. You do get used to it.

On a farm, death and life are not separate things, but each a continuation of the same thing. Still, Rocky had become important to us. He had, in his short time with us, played a huge role in our lives, and we had come to love caring for him. He was such a gracious and enduring creature.

Just as suddenly as Simon had changed into an aggressive and violent animal that we barely knew, he reverted to form and became my Platero again. Animals, I was reminded once more, are never good or bad; they just are what they are. We emotionalize them so much that it is easy to forget this elemental truth.

We missed Rocky — Maria went to his stall every morning and teared up — but to the other animals, the dogs and cats and chickens and donkeys, it was as if he had never been there. Simon didn't so much as glance at Rocky's stall.

Once again, he came up to Maria and me whenever we entered the pasture. He waited to be brushed, scratched, kissed on the nose. His posture changed — he was not as stiff and vigilant, he did not grab his carrots so aggressively, his ears were not always straight up. Whatever threat or danger he perceived from the old pony was gone. It took me longer to recover, I have to say.

It was difficult, for a while, to look at the old worn paths Rocky had made out to the pasture and back to his secret garden. We still expected to hear him whinny when we came into the barn each morning. We closed it off and didn't let the donkeys or the sheep in there.

One consequence of our time with Rocky was that Maria started taking horseback riding lessons. We have acres of woods and trails behind the farmhouse, and I like to think someday she'll have her little pony back, in one way or another.

On some subconscious level, I knew I had felt betrayed. Simon had not only challenged my own notions of him, but he had led us into killing an animal we loved very much. For a few weeks, it was difficult to look at Simon without thinking of that. He didn't mind. He was patient with us.

Time is a great healer, and the rhythms of the farm took over and smoothed things over. The ripples quieted, the tension melted away, our peaceable kingdom returned. We had a lot of animals to take care of, a lot of things to maintain and repair, lots of hay to haul around the barn. In my time owning farms I have learned to respect death. It will come to all of us, no matter how much we fear it and hide from it.

I started reading *Platero and I* to Simon again, and we even took a short walk in the woods behind the farmhouse pasture. Simon seemed to light up when he saw me with the bridle. He needed no prodding to resume our adventures; he held no grudges or bad memories.

Reading the book to him, I saw that I had come to the end, the poignant chapters on Platero's death, and I was struck by how similar the images and feelings were to Simon's first days with me at Bedlam Farm, when he was so near death himself.

Jiménez writes of how he found Platero lying on his bed of straw, eyes soft and sad.

"I went to him, stroked him, talking to him and trying to help him to stand. The poor fellow quivered, started to rise, one forefoot bent under. . . . He could not get up. Then I straightened his foot on the ground, patted him tenderly."

I read this passage over and over again, because it perfectly replicated the first evening Simon spent on my farm, fighting for the strength and breath to stand. I didn't want to let go of that memory, of that bond, and there was no reason to.

I was surprised at how much I had come to love our donkeys, how much they had come to mean to me. In the new farm, the pastures closely ringed the farmhouse, and wherever the animals were, we could see them, and they could see and hear us.

This was a wonderful new dimension to our lives with them. They heard us get up in the morning, and Simon would bray whenever he heard me walking around the house. This was unnerving at times, but I got used to it. Without thinking, I would call out, "Hello, Simon," and I would see him peering in the window by my office, or sometimes outside of the bathroom when I got up in the middle of the night.

He is a sweet soul, Simon, as loyal to me as he is to his ladies.

One night, I wrote him a poem and read it to him:

Simon, you see me, do you not?
Is it not true you see the water running
    through the stream, clear and cold?
Do you not see the deer running through
    the woods?
The children running playfully down the
    road, calling out your name as they
    dance by?

Simon, you do see me.
In the misty sunrise,
In the cloudless dusk,
I hear your bray,
Your call to life,
We are walking together,
Through life.
You do see me, don't you?
How you have opened me up,
I was so closed.
And I see you.

I see more clearly now that Simon is a magical helper, a spirit guide sent to guide me on my hero journey, to help me on my way. He is a teacher who appeared in the form of a donkey. So many animals teach us important lessons if we let them.

And what did he teach me?

To open up, not just to him, not just to animals, but to the human experience. To love, to risk, to friendship. He helped me come so much closer to an understanding of mercy and compassion, something I had been pursuing my whole life.

We are in so many ways a vengeful culture; we are quick to punish wrongdoers and slow to empathize. Simon helped me to see that the farmer was just as piteous as he was, just as damaged. He helped me to open my life up to Red. He brought me closer to Maria, who shared the powerful experience of healing him. He helped me to see that compassion for animals does not mean only keeping them alive but sometimes means letting them go.

He reminded me that mercy and compassion are not only for good people, but also for people who horrify us, upset us, and challenge our notions of humanity. He softened me and my sense of judgment, of righteousness.

Saving a creature is a powerful experience, as so many people who love and support animals know. But the act is most powerful for me when I remember that it is about the animal and not about me. Simon did not ask to be saved, nor does he even understand what that concept means. I do not believe he was grateful to me — he would hardly have driven Rocky into the fence posts if he were — nor does he have any reason to be. By opening myself up to him, I saved myself, taught myself, and challenged myself to think about my life and my world.

Simon's story is not rare; it is all too common. The history of the donkey is rich in cruelty, abandonment, abuse, and neglect. Donkeys are nearly disposable in so many countries, sacrificed to overwork, heat, the lack of food and fresh water. There is something long-suffering about them. Even as I write this, I know that thousands of donkeys have been abandoned in the United States because farmers and others can't afford to care for them. The unusual thing about Simon's story is that he is alive, not that he was mistreated. His great suffering seems so long ago. He is so grounded in his life and at ease here, the king of our little hill.

Simon and I talk once or twice a week now, and we are old soul mates together. He knows what I will do before I do it — he holds his head up to receive the halter when I present it — and I know what he will do before he does it. I pause by the leafy maple trees on our walks so he can eat some leaves.

Red joins us on all of our walks. The two are now as comfortable with each other now as Red was with Rocky. And so the circle of my little triad has closed again in its own way.

I tell Simon of my triumphs and disappointments, and we observe the world together. How ironic, I told him on one recent walk, that I — a boy who grew up reading about strange men walking around with donkeys — should have become one of them.

Simon was not impressed. He was transfixed by a giant white butterfly who rose out of the maple tree and circled around and around over his head.

TWENTY:
OPEN HOUSES, OPEN LIVES

They came from so many different places to see Simon, more than two thousand of them, from California and Canada, Mexico and Maine, South Dakota, Mississippi, and Colorado. They came in their big cars, trucks, and minivans, in their work boots and fancy shoes.

They lined up by the hundreds outside of the big barn to come inside and touch Simon, hug him, give him carrots and cookies, and pepper me with questions about him. For two days I never left the barn. I would ferry one group in to see him and another would form at the gate. Simon, I told him, you are a rock star.

It was humbling to see the wonder, adoration, and affection in their faces, to see the elderly women pushed into the barn in wheelchairs, young and wide-eyed children from New York City and Toronto and Chicago step nervously toward Simon only to discover that he loved every single one of them, loved being touched, hugged, handed cookies and carrots.

His gentleness, especially with children, was poignant. He never grabbed at an apple or carrot, never frightened anyone, never nipped a hand or backed away from being touched or rubbed.

He was the sweetest thing. He was the biggest ham.

For almost all of my eight years there, I had refused visitors at Bedlam Farm. A therapist told me the farm had become a fort, a place to seal off the world. I did not permit visits. I did not welcome the steady stream of cars driving up and down the road, pausing to stare in at the farmhouse, to ooh and aah at the dogs and take photos.

I fully subscribed to the writerly notion of isolation and withdrawal. You wrote your book in peace, came down off of your mountain to do some readings and sign some books, and then you returned. No, I said, this isn't an amusement park. It's a workspace, a private home; we do not permit visitors. It upsets the people, and it upsets the animals. I thought it was rude to be stared at, invaded.

Our first open house had changed all that, and Simon had been the inspiration for it.

This was where the opening up that had begun a year earlier in the very barn where Simon was now greeting his adoring fans had led, widening and deepening and altering my life.

Thanks to the photographs and stories on the blog, Simon had a powerful new story. He was alive and well and thriving. He had walked back from the edge of death and was living life happily and fully. He had me, Maria, Lulu and Fanny, pastures to roam, and people all over the world who loved him.

Six months after we moved, we held another open house at our new farm. Maria organized an art show in her studio, as she had done at the first farm. Simon had long lines of people once more, many of them repeat visitors. He was happy holding court, but the surprise was that I was just as happy. I love showing him off, telling his story and that of all of the donkeys in the world.

With Rocky gone, Simon's reign was complete and unchallenged, his journey a triumph of determination, courage, and the power of love to heal. The creature who had run a blind pony into a fence would stand quietly over children as they kissed him, smacked his nose, and pulled his hair. Compassion takes many forms and shapes, some of them unrecognizable.

Simon's days are filled with ritual and opportunity. He has a pole barn to keep him and his girls, Lulu and Fanny, out of the sun, rain, and snow. He has three pastures filled with the brush, apple trees, streams, and ravines that donkeys love to wander in and explore. We visit him several times a day. Maria brushes him and sings to him in the morning. I bring him equine cookies, apples, carrots, bread, and pasta, which he loves. Every morning, Lulu or Fanny — sometimes both — kick him in one side of the head or the other; it doesn't seem to bother him. He has gotten over his difficulties with Ken Norman, and submits to having his hooves trimmed.

Simon's twisted legs are the only remaining sign of his many injuries. I think cold weather is hard on his legs, and I sometimes see him lie down in reluctant resignation, something healthy donkeys rarely do.

Although he is best known and well known for his mistreatment, there is no sign that he recollects it in any way, or carries any behavioral scars. There is no type of human — man, woman, old, young — that he fears or shies away from. I can only assume his mistreatment was episodic, not chronic; he has no wariness or mistrust of people.

I will never forget the long lines of people

who traveled from all across the country to see Simon. They helped me understand the power of animals to touch our hearts and change our lives.

Saint Thomas Aquinas got it right, I think, and my experience with Simon taught me that compassion is not an easy or a pretty thing — not in animals, not in people.

Simon did not save me, I saved him, but he did teach me what compassion is all about. How hard compassion is, and how easy it is to withhold it from people I don't like, or who do cruel or offensive things. The true pilgrim, the real seeker of compassion, learns to cross such bridges; each one is different and leads us to a different place.

Simon touches the deepest parts of me; it is such a joy to give him the life he deserves. He lovingly accepts the person I am. He challenges me to become the person I want to be.

Epilogue:
Toward a
Compassionate Heart

In the spring of 2013, I began studying Tai Chi, the Chinese practice of movement and meditation. One day when I was feeling particularly unsettled, I walked through the pasture, into the barn, stood still and began my movements there.

Simon, attuned to me as always, came over and stood quietly by my side. As I moved my arms in a circle and looked up at the sky, I felt a gentle pressure in my back. Simon had pressed his head against my spine, and for the next ten minutes, I leaned back against him, practicing my movements, feeling his support and connection.

It was a profoundly spiritual moment, an experience that showed me just how close an animal can be to a human he knows and feels safe around. I felt that Simon completely understood what I was doing in my practice, and helped me to achieve the calm and peacefulness I was seeking. Perhaps it helped him as well.

The news of the world is filled with cruelty and violence; we are forced to confront it all day, almost every day. Troubling stories are no longer compartmentalized in the morning paper or on the evening news. They permeate our lives, our homes, our work spaces, the very air we breathe. They are no longer occasional disturbances, but now part of the ether.

It is difficult to feel compassion for the people we see and read and hear about doing the most awful things. Our civic life is filled with strife and argument rather than comfort and guidance.

Every day, we are called upon to forgive and understand behavior that is sometimes beyond our comprehension and challenges our ideas about compassion.

Jesus, Thomas Merton, Albert Schweitzer, and the Dalai Lama can say what they want about compassion; most people do not accept their messages, do not believe we are all one and the same. Most of our institutions are not built on empathy. Compassion is tricky, dangerous, volatile. It is easy to talk about it, but another thing to practice it. Simon had taught me that. But he also taught me not to give up on it.

The Lincolns, Gandhis, Martin Luther

Kings, and Nelson Mandelas of the world are much admired, but if you look at their mostly common fates — we tend to either kill or exile them — their practice of compassion was perceived to be dangerous. Why would any normal human being choose that fate?

Donkeys have always represented the best and worst of the human experience, loved, celebrated in great art, revered, reviled, abandoned, and mistreated. They have always walked with human beings in the theater of chance, as Simon was walking with me.

There is a wonderful simplicity to compassion, as Simon helped me understand that afternoon. All you need to do is ask yourself this: what kind of a person do you want to be?

Months later, a priest, the codirector of a Catholic boys orphanage in Brooklyn, called me. The group, Father Joseph said, was coming upstate to spend a few days at a retreat. A reader of my blog, he thought it would be wonderful for the boys to meet some farm animals and to see Red herd sheep.

Most of the boys knew dogs only as guard animals; they had no concept of pets. But mainly, he said, he thought they ought to meet Simon. The priest sensed his gentleness from my photos and stories about him.

He warned me that most of the boys had come from extraordinarily difficult backgrounds. Some were the victims of rape and incest. Others had been arrested by the police for different crimes. Some were the children of illegal immigrants or had been abandoned when their parents had died, gotten sick, or just vanished.

Some had severe emotional and behavioral problems; he hoped I would be comfortable with that.

Father Joseph added that only one of the boys — a young teenager from Mexico — had ever seen a farm animal; he had grown up with a donkey. The priest told me he was especially drawn to the idea that a spirit can suffer awful misfortune and keep an open heart. He thought that might be the message of Simon, one the boys could empathize with and perhaps emulate.

I agreed to the visit. A few days later two battered vans pulled into the farm's driveway, and about twenty boys and five or six counselors and priests hopped out.

Father Joseph had not misrepresented the group or exaggerated their troubles. They were all children of color — black, Latino,

Asian. Some could barely speak and had obvious emotional disorders and physical disabilities.

I admired Father Joseph, the priest who had called me and now stood grinning in my backyard. He had a warm smile, and his patience and affection for the boys was palpable. This was somebody who didn't need any lessons in compassion; he was all about it. Although some of the boys challenged him, refused to come when called, or talked over him, he never wavered in his calm and affectionate responses and eventually got everybody to do what needed to be done.

Lenore and Red greeted the boys enthusiastically, tails wagging. Most of the boys were clearly afraid of dogs. I remembered Father Joseph's caution about their unfamiliarity with animals and called the dogs off, making them stand back until the visitors could get used to them.

Jean, a seventeen-year-old Haitian orphan whose family was killed in that country's devastating earthquake, was the first to step forward and put his hand on Red's head. Red, now a licensed therapy dog, stood still and looked Jean in the eye. The other boys were astonished. It seemed they had never seen a dog quite like Red, and, one by one, most of them followed Jean's example.

I noticed that Simon had appeared outside the pole barn and had walked over to the gate. Simon understood the concept of visitors, and his gaze fell on Father Joseph and the other counselors, who were holding large bags of carrots.

Simon looked over the group carefully and let out a joyous and welcoming bray that sent several boys running back to the vans.

No, no, this is Simon's welcome, I explained. This is how he says hello.

Another boy named Juan walked up to the gate. Father Joseph whispered to me that his family had been murdered in front of him in a Bronx drug war; he had never seen the ocean or a farm. The boy came up to me and shook my hand and asked me in broken but intelligible English to tell Simon's story to the group, which I did. I told the story of Simon's mistreatment on the farm and gave a brief synopsis of the history of donkeys. I discussed what they eat, how long they live, and how to approach them and touch them.

Then I opened the gate and invited them all to come into the pasture and stand in a semicircle around the donkeys. The counselors and I broke up the carrots into little pieces and handed chunks to those boys who wanted to get closer — only four or five did.

Simon was an intuitive host; it was always hard to reconcile his troubled story with his gentle nature. He was good at reading people; he never approached people who were nervous around him.

For ten minutes or so, one member of the group after another stepped forward with their hands out and Simon crunched away at the carrots he had come to expect from visitors.

Juan stayed back; he was clearly frightened of the big donkey, unwilling to get close or to offer him a carrot.

Simon had a ring of people around him — counselors and kids — holding their carrots out, but something drew him to Juan, who stood back by the gate. Simon walked through the circle and toward Juan, who was holding Father Joseph's hand and watching wide-eyed.

"It's okay," I said, moving toward them. "He won't hurt you." I trusted Simon completely, but I wasn't certain what he wanted from Juan. Simon stood alongside of the boy. He looked down at his bright green sneakers, shook his head a bit, and leaned down to sniff them — perhaps he thought they were food.

Then he simply stood alongside the boy, staring out through the gate.

"What does he want?" asked Juan nervously.

"He is waiting for you to rub or scratch his ears," I said.

There was a long silence. The other boys were all standing still, holding their carrots and watching. Then some of them began offering opinions about what Simon wanted — he wanted food, he wanted a walk, he wanted to say hello.

After a while, I saw Juan's hand slowly come out and scratch Simon right below his ears, one of his favorite scratching spots. Simon stood stock still, his lips trembling, as happens when donkeys are content; it's like a cat purring.

Simon waited, rooted to the ground. Juan rubbed his nose, then asked for some carrots to offer him. He reached out nervously, holding his palm open as we had suggested. Simon gingerly reached over and took the carrot, chewing it thoughtfully and carefully. Juan, still holding Father Joseph's hand, began stroking Simon along the side of his neck.

Some of the other boys came over; they all petted Simon and gave him their remaining carrots. We then took the group out of

Simon's pasture to the other side of the farmhouse to watch Red herd the sheep. Juan asked if he could stay behind and be with Simon, and one of the counselors agreed to stay behind with him. I said it was fine.

Red and I did our sheepherding-for-visitors show. The boys were mesmerized; none of them had ever seen a dog as responsive or agile as Red, and the idea that he could control the sheep seemed to fascinate them.

At the end of the demonstration, Father Joseph took my arm and walked me out into the yard where I could see Simon and Juan standing at the gate, and he pointed to them.

Juan was standing in front of Simon, his forehead pressing against the contented donkey. Simon and the boy seemed to be lost in their own world, communicating in a powerful and emotional way — a way I could not have imagined just a few months earlier.

"You cannot imagine what a gift this is for Juan," Father Joseph told me, and then he smiled. "What a compassionate heart your donkey has."

A NOTE TO THE READER

If you would like to see Simon bray, we have a video for you online: https://www.youtube.com/watch?v= sdDYQ6bcdow.

ABOUT THE AUTHOR

Jon Katz has written twenty-six books, including works of nonfiction, novels, short stories, and books for children; he is also a photographer. He has written for *The New York Times, The Wall Street Journal, Slate, Rolling Stone,* and the *AKC Gazette,* and has worked for CBS News, *The Boston Globe, The Washington Post,* and *The Philadelphia Inquirer.* He lives on Bedlam Farm, in upstate New York, with his wife, the artist Maria Wulf, and their dogs, donkeys, barn cats, sheep, and chickens.

www.bedlamfarm.com
Facebook.com/AuthorJonKatz
@katzinbedlam